Unexpected Destinations

Unexpected Destinations

The Poignant Story of Japan's First Vassar Graduate

Akiko Kuno

Translated by *Kirsten McIvor*

KODANSHA INTERNATIONAL
Tokyo New York London

Originally published in Japanese by Chuokoronsha as *Rokumeikan no kifujin: Oyama Sutematsu*.

Distributed in the United States by Kodansha America, Inc., 114 Fifth Avenue, New York, N.Y. 10011, and in the United Kingdom and continental Europe by Kodansha Europe Ltd., Gillingham House, 38-44 Gillingham Street, London SW1V 1HU. Published by Kodansha International Ltd., 17-14 Otowa 1-chome, Bunkyo-ku, Tokyo 112, and Kodansha America, Inc.

93 94 95 10 9 8 7 6 5 4 3 2 1
ISBN 4-7700-1638-7

Library of Congress Cataloging-in-Publication Data

Kuno, Akiko, 1940–
    [Rokumeikan no kifujin Oyama Sutematsu. English]
    Unexpected destinations : the poignant story of Japan's first Vassar graduate / by Akiko Kuno ; translated by Kirsten McIvor. —1st ed.
        p.   cm.
    Isbn 4–7700–1638–7
    1. Oyama, Sutematsu, 1860–1919.   2. Oyama, Iwao, 1842–1916. 3. Wives—Japan—Biography.   4. Japanese students—United States—Biography. I. Title.
DS884.08908613 1993
952.03'1'092—dc20
[B]
92–44890
CIP

CONTENTS

Preface

This book is based on nearly forty letters addressed to "Dear Alice," which my great-grandmother, Sutematsu Oyama, one of the first Japanese female students to study abroad and the first to graduate from an American college, wrote from Japan to her American host sister Alice Bacon. Lying on my desk in my home in Tokyo right now is one of those letters, written by Sutematsu shortly after she decided to marry the minister of war, Iwao Oyama, barely six months after her return home. The letter is back in Japan 110 years after it had been carried by steamer to the United States in July 1883. Neither the ink nor the stationery has faded, and I can almost hear Sutematsu breathing as I gaze at it.

In Japan I found little information about Sutematsu, and what I did manage to unearth was of little use, most references being either vague or erroneous. On the rare occasion when she was mentioned, it was usually in comparison with Umeko Tsuda, a compatriot who also studied in the United States during the same period. While Umeko Tsuda is well known for having founded Tsuda College, the first of its kind for women in Japan, Sutematsu is frequently dismissed, criticized as having done nothing of any significance after she returned to Japan, despite having been a government-sponsored student for eleven years. Those accounts of her activities which do exist tend to emphasize her seemingly glamorous life as a member of the upper classes. Little is written of the other uses she made of her experience abroad, particularly in strengthening Japan-U.S. relations.

Sutematsu was a member of the aristocracy, yes, but she was more. If Sutematsu had chosen the path of a single career woman—as Umeko Tsuda did—her life would be of less interest to me. Umeko had possessed an iron will, and indeed made outstanding contributions to Japanese society. Sutematsu, too, made her contributions, but in an entirely different way. The life choices she made as a turn-of-the-century returnee to Japan begged for more exploration.

Here was an intelligent and beautiful Japanese woman, Vassar class president and valedictorian, who was ready and willing to offer Japan a cosmopolitan and educated view of the West, if only her countrymen would make use of her talents. As it turned out, Japan wasn't ready for Sutematsu. Rather than dedicate her life single-mindedly to the higher education of women, which she knew in all probability would have entailed a life filled with struggle and loneliness, Sutematsu chose to balance the conventional desires of any average woman of the day—marriage and family—with the talents she had acquired during her study in America. As we can now understand from contemporary experience, Sutematsu's choice was in many ways more difficult, for it required a constant balancing act: bringing up a large family, keeping the necessary low profile required of a woman married into fame and status, and sustaining her stubborn desire to be of service to a country still mired in feudalistic trappings.

Sutematsu is also an attractive figure because of her essential vulnerability. She was already at an age ripe for marriage when she returned to her country (Umeko Tsuda was younger by about five years), and yet finding a husband had not been her major concern. How she negotiated the social pressures and limitations imposed upon her, and how she adapted the dreams of her American youth is the story I was able to uncover. If in presenting her story—much of it based on letters stored away for over one hundred years in a small town in America—I can help the reader gain an understanding of the challenges facing this remarkable woman, then I will consider that my aim in writing the book has been fulfilled.

I know that Nucy Meech and Grace Case, who made it possible for me to find the letters, historian Bernard Heinz and the staff of the Alumni and Alumnae of Vassar College who provided so much useful material, Jill Bryant who took such care to preserve the letters and photographs, and a host of other friends I made through my research have been eagerly awaiting the publication of this English edition. I hope they will accept it as an expression of my gratitude for their invaluable assistance in compiling my great-grandmother's story. I also hope that in some small way it will help to increase the understanding between our two nations.

Akiko Kuno
Tokyo, Japan

UNEXPECTED DESTINATIONS

Retracing My Great-Grandmother's Steps

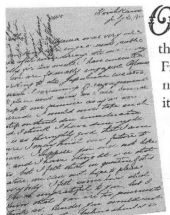

On July 21, 1982, I contemplated the Pacific stretching out below me from the window of my plane bound for San Francisco. The ocean was living up to its name that day. Hardly a wave disturbed its glassy surface.

Those deceptively tame waters had, almost exactly one hundred years earlier, tossed the American steamship *Arabic* mercilessly about as it crossed the other way, from the United States to Japan. Among the passengers on that voyage were two young Japanese women, impeccably dressed in the Western fashions of the day. They were Sutematsu Yamakawa and Umeko Tsuda, whose parents had responded to a recruitment by the Japanese government to send them to America eleven years previously, despite the opposition of many Japanese who believed that they were abandoning their daughters to some unspeakable fate in a barbaric land.

Since my childhood days I had occasionally heard mention of my great-grandmother, who, relations told me, was one of Japan's first five female students to study abroad. During those years Sutematsu was to me no more than an ancestor who figured in my father's and grandmother's stories of earlier days, mainly for the fact that she spoke English better than she did Japanese. Why had Sutematsu been entrusted at the age of eleven with the important mission of studying in a foreign country and becoming a model for future Japanese women? How did she cope with a completely different culture without prior knowledge of English? What kind of family did she stay with? When she returned to Japan why did she rush into a marriage with the minister of war, a man eighteen years older than herself? Sutematsu was viewed as a celebrated beauty in the early years after her return, during the period in which Japanese high society revolved around events at the Rokumeikan pavilion, which was the setting for high-ranking Japanese and Westerners to mingle at ostensibly Western social functions, but how did she really make use of her overseas experience during that period, and for the remaining years of her married life? Those were questions that, even as an adult, I never thought to ask about my great-grandmother, who had played such a special role in Japan's history during the turbulent Meiji period.

I was aroused from this lack of interest in Sutematsu in the spring of 1980, when I was enjoying a chat with an American friend after a game of tennis. Nucy Meech had come to Japan ten years earlier in connection with her husband's work, and I had met her through CWAJ (College Women's Association of Japan), an international volunteer organization comprised of female university graduates. She was an excellent tennis player, and despite her being twenty-some years my senior—she was over sixty—I never managed to beat her.

I recall that our conversation concerned Japanese women educated in America and their problems in finding work and getting married on their return to Japan. Mrs. Meech wondered aloud when the first Japanese woman had graduated from an American university, and who she had been.

I informed her that the first Japanese female graduated from an

American university a hundred years ago, and that she was in fact my great-grandmother, Sutematsu Yamakawa.

"That's marvelous!" my companion exclaimed. "You must be very proud to have such a woman for a great-grandmother." "Tell me more," she added, leaning forward eagerly. However, to my embarrassment I was unable to answer most of her questions.

My tennis partner's curiosity regarding Sutematsu did not end that day. Unbeknown to me, Mrs. Meech wrote to Vassar College, Sutematsu's alma mater, and several months later a fat yellow envelope from the office of Alumni and Alumnae of Vassar College (AAVC) turned up on my doorstep. Inside were photocopies of several articles related to Sutematsu that had appeared in American newspapers over the years, each labelled "Vassar Class of '82." Among them was an article Sutematsu herself had written—about her impressions of Japan after an eleven-year absence—and there was an interview conducted by an American reporter after Sutematsu had married Iwao Oyama, in which she gave a vivid account of her childhood memories of the Aizu War. Yet another set of articles written by Sutematsu during the Russo-Japanese War informed the American public of the efforts Japanese women were making on the home front to support their men fighting overseas.

With the delivery of these documents an image of Sutematsu began to form in my mind, an image of somebody other than just "my great-grandmother." For the first time I saw her as a woman who had left Japan's shores to become one of the first of her sex to be entrusted with the important mission of gaining knowledge of the West—at an exciting turning point in Japanese history. At the same time I resolved to find out about her formative years in the United States, and to see for myself her adopted home of New Haven and the college where she had studied. A hundred years had passed since Sutematsu had left New Haven, but I felt it was not too late to retrace her steps.

Thus began my correspondence with the office of Alumni and Alumnae of Vassar College. In Japan, I soon discovered, there was a dearth of material dealing with Sutematsu's youth. She was mentioned only briefly in the records of the Iwakura Mission with which she had traveled abroad in 1871 and in the history of Tsuda College, a school founded by one of her compatriots who had also studied in America. Due greatly to the dedication and enthusiasm of AAVC, however, I managed to start putting together an account of my great-grandmother's years in the United States. As well as the aforementioned articles, the office provided me with a number of photographs, among the most memorable of which was a picture taken of Sutematsu after her graduation, looking splendid in a beautiful white gown, and another of her in Japanese court robe during her visit to the imperial palace on returning home.

The material I received from Vassar, however, dealt only with Sutematsu's time there and events after her return to Japan, and gave me virtually no clues regarding her life with the Bacon family, in whose home she had spent the first six years of her stay. Accordingly, I arranged with the association to place the following advertisement in their magazine, the *Vassar Quarterly*:

> **Seeking Memories of a Princess.** Sutematsu Yamakawa, later Princess Oyama, who graduated from Vassar in 1882 as valedictorian of her class, is thought to be the first Japanese woman to be educated outside of Japan. Because of her importance in the history of Japanese women, her great-granddaughter is trying to write a book to preserve her story for future generations and seeks to meet or hear from descendants of the class of 1882. Any information should be sent to: Akiko Kuno, 1-29-19-204, Miyanosaka, Setagaya-ku, Tokyo, Japan.

Unfortunately, obtaining the information I required was not as simple as placing the advertisement. A year passed with no word from America, and I began to think that the one-century gap between the young Sutematsu and me was too wide to bridge. Then, just when I felt I had exhausted all avenues of inquiry, a letter containing a small pamphlet arrived in the mail.

The envelope bore a New Haven postmark, and the sender was a Grace Case. Mrs. Case, who had graduated from Vassar fifty-five years earlier, wrote that on reading my article in the *Quarterly* she had visited the archives at Yale and had found the letters and diaries of the Reverend Leonard Bacon, in whose household Sutematsu lived for six years, as well as the pamphlet—a history of the churches in New Haven—written by local historian Bernard Heinz. Both authors mentioned the young Japanese girl in their writings. That kindly written letter from across the Pacific gave me the clues I needed to begin earnestly researching the years between Sutematsu's arrival in New Haven and her time at Vassar College. My joy was compounded when shortly after I received another letter, this time from Bernard Heinz himself. Mr. Heinz informed me that Yale University held a number of documents explaining the circumstances by which Sutematsu had come to live with the Bacon family, and that Alfred Bacon, the reverend's grandson, was alive and well.

A month later a letter arrived from Alfred Bacon's daughter, Jill Bryant. In it she explained that a large number of letters Sutematsu wrote to the reverend's youngest daughter Alice over a forty-year period had been carefully stored away by the family. I could hardly have hoped for better news. The time had come for me to go to America, sift through all the material, and see with my own eyes the town where Sutematsu had lived and the college she had attended.

It was not without reservations that I considered the trip. I had spent a year at Hope College in Michigan during the early sixties, a time when the United States was truly the world's "number one" country in every sense of the word: the economy was thriving and hope was in the air. I would be returning to a country where Japanese cars monopolized the roads, and where products bearing "Made in Japan" stickers had infiltrated people's lives. Trade friction was causing a deterioration of the amicable feelings of Americans toward Japan, and I was therefore a little apprehensive at the thought of uprooting my ten-year-old son and taking off to the States to follow Sutematsu's trail on the strength of a few letters. In the end, however, I decided it was too late to abandon the project I had begun. Putting my trust in the new acquaintances whom I knew only through correspondence about Sutematsu, I prepared for the trip. Mrs. Case kindly arranged for my son to attend a summer camp near New Haven, and the day after school let out we boarded a flight bound for San Francisco.

> On the morning of our arrival, we sailed through fog so thick we could barely see what lay before us. Finally the ship was forced to anchor and we stood on the slippery deck, waiting for daybreak. As the cloud lifted we were greeted by a spectacular view of the mountains of California, while in the bay steamships plied back and forth puffing out smoke by the bridge known as the 'Golden Gate.'

This passage is from the chapter "San Francisco," in the journal *Beio Kairan Jikki*, an account of the 1872 Iwakura Mission to the United States and Europe written by Kunitake Kume, an official from the Foreign Ministry. In *Beio Kairan Jikki*, America and Americans are seen through the eyes of someone whose country had only recently emerged from a long isolation. Kume's account is fresh and lively, and meticulously detailed. During my own stay in America I kept a paperback copy of the slender volume with me at all times, because whenever possible I wanted to visit the same places that Sutematsu had visited with the members of the mission. Kume had recorded the day's weather, time of day, and the date as well as places; those dates proved invaluable when I began researching local press reports on the visitors from the "land of the Mikado." Without Kume's journal it would have been almost impossible for me to sort through the vast amounts of microfilmed material that I found in the libraries of every town I visited.

In San Francisco I made my way to the public library several days in a row and read on microfilm newspaper articles from over a hundred years ago. Perhaps it was the mission's novelty value, or because San Francisco was its first port of call, but in any case almost every local paper seemed to cover the visitors' day-to-day activities in depth. Many of the articles showed a profound lack of knowledge about Japan, and it was with a wry smile that I read some of the writers' blatantly biased observations about their guests. The Japanese males were dismissed as being too short and without many redeeming features at all, a far cry from the mighty "samurai" whom Americans had envisaged. The five female students, however, were likened to dolls in their beautiful kimonos, hailed as charming, and were loved wherever they went.

It took the members of the Iwakura Mission a month to cross the United States by train, during which time they were plagued by heavy snows. My son and I flew from San Francisco to New York in only five hours. From there a two-hour bus ride brought us to Sutematsu's second home: New Haven, Connecticut. I had imagined a sleepy university town in a quiet pastoral setting, so when we actually reached New Haven, I was quite surprised. Huge freighters and fishing boats lay at anchor in the harbor to the east of the town, connected to the center by a railway line, and modern banks and department stores competed for the attention of shoppers around the historic buildings of Yale University. It was already dark, but the streets still resounded with the chatter of students and the roar of motorbikes. Eventually we arrived at the bus terminal, and I dragged my tired son into a taxi and gave the driver Mrs. Case's address, which I had long since memorized.

My first meeting with Grace Case swept away any reservations I had harbored about coming to New Haven. On our arrival at her apartment building we found the elderly lady sitting on a sofa in the lobby, reading and waiting patiently for us, even though we were almost two hours late. Without thinking my son and I simultaneously exclaimed, "That's Mrs. Case!" at which the white-haired figure rose, smiling, and embraced us both in a powerful hug. I will never forget the warmth of that welcome, which belied the fact that the connection between us was anything as tenuous as an interest in a woman who had happened to live in the town a hundred years before.

Mrs. Case explained that her husband, a professor of English literature at Yale, had died about twenty years ago, and that thanks to his provision for her she was able to live comfortably in her own apartment, one of a complex of such residences for the elderly. We sat nibbling the sandwiches she had made and forgot the time as we chatted about Sutematsu, Vassar College, and the town of New Haven. During the conversation our hostess kept returning to one point: that one must never lose one's curiosity or thirst for knowledge. It was words to that effect, written in a letter, that had persuaded me to make the trip; if Mrs. Case herself had not possessed those very qualities, the facts about Sutematsu's youth would have remained buried forever.

The next day we drove to the nearby summer camp, which was located on the shore of a beautiful lake. Mrs. Case's driving was a little hair-raising at times, but we arrived safely, and after depositing my son, the two of us went on to a colonial-style restaurant for lunch. Our final destination was the home of historian Bernard Heinz. "I would love to spend more time with you," Mrs. Case said, "but you should stay with Mr. Heinz now. He knows a great deal about New Haven history, and you'll learn far more from him than by being with me." She embraced and kissed me as we said our goodbyes.

Mr. Heinz, a stout man who looked to be in his early sixties, lived with his wife in the New Haven suburb of Guilford. As a freelance writer he penned articles related to local history for newspapers and magazines. His wife had taught religious studies at Vassar College.

In the center of New Haven lies an open space known as "The Green." Three churches stand on it, all built approximately 160 years ago. The mystery of why three churches should be standing in such a small area had aroused Bernard Heinz's curiosity, prompting him to move to New Haven, where he could conduct his research closer at hand. During his investigations he found mention of Leonard Bacon, minister of Center Church (which stood, not surprisingly, in the middle of The Green), and of the young Japanese girl living in the minister's home.

The five days I stayed at the Heinz home were spent locating material related to Sutematsu. Mr. Heinz arranged for a special pass that enabled me to use the Yale library and archives freely, and I spent every day from nine in the morning until closing at five tracking down records of the Bacon family. There was an incredible volume of information concerning the Reverend Leonard Bacon, including books he had authored, antislavery articles from newspapers, and several dozen diaries written over the course of his eighty-year life. Concentrating on the six years from 1872 to 1878, during which time Sutematsu had lived with the family, I painstakingly read every piece concerning her. I was thrilled when I discovered the brief note "October 31, 1872—Two Japanese girls came today" in one of the musty diaries, and felt as if my great-grandmother was congratulating me on having come thus far.

In his spare time Mr. Heinz showed me around New Haven. His knowledge of the town was even greater than I had imagined. He brought its history to life so vividly, including that of individual buildings, that I almost believed he had been there a hundred years ago to see things with his own eyes. Sutematsu was very fortunate to have been sent here, he explained. Aided by the establishment of Yale University in 1718, throughout its history New Haven had enjoyed a high level of education and cultural activities. The progressive nature of the town was also evident in the number of educational facilities for women that had been standing since the early nineteenth century. Therefore, the historian concluded, the area had long been home to a large number of well-educated and independent women unfettered by domestic chains. The youngest of the Bacon children, Alice (two years older than Sutematsu), was unable to attend college for economic reasons, but passed the advanced Harvard examinations for women purely through her own study. In later years Alice was to come to Japan to assist in women's education, in response to the pleas of Sutematsu and Umeko Tsuda.

I left Mrs. Case and the Heinzes and continued on my way, taking a train from New York that followed the Hudson River upstream to Poughkeepsie, and Vassar College. Poughkeepsie is a quiet college town of seventy thousand, set among what seemed a never-ending succession of rolling green hills. Mary Gesek, associate director of AAVC, the organization with which I had been corresponding for two years, was waiting at the station with her husband to pick me up. She suggested that we take a tour of the college by car, as I probably wanted to see the campus where Sutematsu had studied before I did anything else.

The faded red brick and grey stone buildings nestled comfortably among shady trees, much as they had 120 years earlier when Vassar was opened. It was here that Sutematsu spent what she later described as the happiest four years of her life. That evening Mrs. Gesek and the staff of the AAVC office held a welcome party for me. The other staff members were mainly recent graduates, but their enthusiasm and obvious pride in Sutematsu surprised me.

The next day I entered the library to find an impressive pile of material laid out on the tables waiting for me. There were photographs of Sutematsu's thirty-eight Vassar classmates, letters she had written them, notices written in French informing them of her marriage to Iwao Oyama, a postcard depicting Oyama and Admiral Togo with the emperor during the Russo-Japanese War. . . . All of it was new to me, and I could not help but be impressed by the association's diligence in preserving these pieces of history for over a hundred years. Their dedicated efforts, combined with the results of the abiding attachment Sutematsu had felt for her old school till the end of her days, had provided me with a surprisingly comprehensive collection of material. It seemed to me that despite America's relatively short history, or perhaps because of it, Americans take a far greater interest in their family records than Japanese people do. This interest in preserving records of the past was evident everywhere I visited during my stay, including the local libraries, where I found a wealth of information stored.

Jill Bryant came to see me after I had been at Vassar three days, driving doggedly through one of Poughkeepsie's infamous summer storms to pick me up at the college. She had taken time off from her library job near Philadelphia to drive me to Cornwall, Connecticut, her father's home. Jill had piercing eyes and chestnut brown hair, streaked with white, that was tied in a neat bun; she was the spitting image of her great-aunt Alice Bacon. Alice was the main person in whom throughout her life, Sutematsu had confided her innermost thoughts. Jill's father was eighty-seven years old and almost blinded by cataracts, but, she told me, he had clear memories of his Aunt Alice.

We set off, driving through thickly forested hills and over a suspension bridge, then followed a little-used road through a sparsely populated farming area. Here and there could be seen the remains of army campsites from the Revolutionary War. On our arrival at the two-hundred-year-old Bacon family home in the village of Cornwall, we found our host sitting in a rocking chair. The elderly Yale graduate had put on a necktie for his visitors' benefit, despite the blistering heat, and when we reached him he extended a large friendly hand and in his mannerly way welcomed me, impressed by how I'd come all the way from Japan.

In the bedroom I was to use stood a chest of drawers that Alice had brought back from Japan. The wooden bed, itself over a hundred years old, was covered with a clean quilted bedspread. The floor, which had been trodden on by successive occupants of the room for two hundred-years, had a black luster and was slightly uneven in places. All in all it was the perfect setting to study the events of a hundred years ago.

In contrast to the daytime heat the nights were cool, so Alfred Bacon and I positioned ourselves by the log fire for our talks. Occasionally reaching over to throw on a log, the old gentleman told me what he had heard from his Aunt Alice about Sutematsu and as well as about life in New Haven in those days. He spoke slowly and carefully so that I could easily understand. To my delight, when Sutematsu appeared in one of his stories it was always as a daughter of the family, rather than as "the Oriental student from abroad."

The letters I had been eagerly waiting to see were carefully stored in a large wooden chest, along with an Arita pottery coffee set and organdy tablecloth Sutematsu had sent the family, and a kimono that Alice is said to have greatly loved. Sutematsu began her correspondence with Alice on her return to Japan and kept it up until Alice's death at the age of sixty, sharing her troubles and joys with her beloved elder sister for almost forty years. Unable to read or write proficiently in Japanese for the rest of her days, it was in English that Sutematsu could best express her feelings.

The forty precious letters included those that were written by Sutematsu soon after her return to Japan, in which she expressed her disgust at the persistence of old customs and her frustration with many aspects of Japanese society. Others speak of a love affair—an aspect of her life I had never known about. Many of the letters contained insights into historical incidents that could only have been gained by the wife of an important government functionary. I realized it was unthinkable for such valuable documents to remain sleeping in a chest in the Bacon home forever. As it turned out, Mrs. Bryant had been thinking along the same lines and had contacted the Library of Congress with the intention of donating the letters. I was duty-bound as Sutematsu's descendant to publish them in Japan, she told me, and after painstakingly typing each one so that it was easier to read before my visit, she passed them on to me along with photocopies of the originals. I had actually been undecided up to that point about writing Sutematsu's biography, but now I knew without a doubt what I needed to do with the material I had collected.

After four days of enjoying the Bacons' hospitality, I left for the town of New Brunswick, New Jersey, to visit the library of Rutgers University. I have to admit that the university's name was unknown to me until I started my investigations, but as I began to read in-depth about the Japanese who went to study abroad from the end of the feudal era through the first years of the Meiji period, I realized the importance of the role played by the university in the formation of modern Japan, and particularly of the Iwakura Mission.

With the first appearance of Commodore Perry's "black ships" in Uraga Bay in Edo (modern-day Tokyo), the race to learn from the West had begun. The various domains competed furiously with each other to find out all they could about Western politics, economics, and education from the American missionaries who arrived soon after. Christianity was still banned by the shogunate, so the missionaries had to be content with passing on knowledge of a more worldly nature to their eager pupils. Several future leaders of the Meiji Restoration government, including Hirobumi Ito, Toshimichi Okubo, and Shigenobu Okuma, studied English and other subjects from one of those missionaries, Dr. G. Verbeck, who had maintained close ties with Rutgers through the Dutch Reformed Church in Nagasaki, with which he was affiliated. In 1869 he persuaded Okuma, then responsible for foreign affairs, that Japan needed to learn as much as it could from the West, and as quickly as possible. The detailed plan he submitted for an overseas study tour became the basic foundation for the Iwakura Mission to the United States and Europe two years later.

Rutgers College (the State University of New Jersey), originally Queen's College, was founded in 1766 by members of the Dutch Reformed Church. The first Japanese students, the Yokoi brothers, Saheita and Tahei, were sent to Rutgers in 1866 with the secret assistance of Verbeck, in defiance of the shogunate's ban on overseas travel. As members of the Higo domain on Kyushu island in southern Japan, the brothers' mission was to study Western shipbuilding and gunsmithing techniques and bring their knowledge back to Japan. The young men's English ability was naturally considerably lower than the level required for understanding university lectures, so for the first few months of their stay they joined pupils of Rutgers Preparatory School for lessons. Saheita subsequently entered the U.S. Naval Academy at Annapolis, but failed to pass the graduation examination; Tahei entered Rutgers College, only to return to Japan in 1870 on account of ill health, without completing his degree.

The visit of the Yokoi brothers paved the way for others, and

Japanese students followed each other in rapid succession to the town of New Brunswick: forty by the time of the Meiji Restoration and over three hundred by 1880. It is a little-known fact that a large proportion of the high-ranking officials in the Meiji government studied at Rutgers in their younger days. It must be said, however, that only three actually completed degrees. Sutematsu's brother Kenjiro also began his overseas experience at Rutgers, but finding it too full of his countrymen and therefore hardly conducive to learning English, he moved to Norwich, Connecticut, and continued his studies there. Japanese students in New Brunswick generally managed somehow to obtain lodgings in the homes of local people friendly to Japan, but it was no simple matter, for even the poor Irish maids of potential hosts had a habit of leaving when they found out a Japanese was coming to stay.

The traffic was not all one-way. At least ten American graduates of the college made their way to Japan immediately before and after the Meiji Restoration to take up advisory positions in the new government. Robert Pruyn, appointed by Lincoln to be America's first minister to Japan, James Ballagh, founder of the Reformed Church in Japan, and the chemist William Griffis, the first highly paid foreigner to be employed by the Meiji government, were all members of this group.

My guide in New Brunswick was Professor Emeritus Ardath W. Burks at Rutgers University. Professor Burks specialized in the study of those special salaried foreigners employed by the Meiji government to help modernize Japan, and had a particular interest in the Griffis Collection of material concerning Japanese students, which was kept in the university's library. I arrived to find that he had already delved into the Collection and had prepared photocopies of material he thought relevant to my research.

Enjoying lunch in the faculty dining room, I contemplated how difficult life must have been for those Japanese students in New Brunswick. During their studies, some fell ill and died, having been unable to return home because of their illegal exit from Japan. Those unfortunate young men are buried in a corner of the public cemetery christened "Willow Grove" by the locals. A visit there revealed nine gravestones, the names still legible if severely eroded by a hundred years of wind and rain. Most had died around the year 1870, and all had been in their early twenties. Nearby willow trees stood guard over the graves, and as I listened, the sound of the wind rushing through them was transformed into the lamenting voices of those students. I found myself putting my hands together in prayer for them.

New Brunswick was the final stop on my itinerary of places that played a significant part in the lives of Sutematsu and her peers in the United States. A hundred years had passed since a little girl from far-away Japan came to America, living and studying for more than ten years, but there was a surprising wealth of information to be found concerning her stay and subsequent life in Japan; in fact, I was deeply impressed by the diligent record-keeping of enthusiasts in every town I visited. To Sutematsu's own credit, had she been a less intelligent and friendly young woman I doubt she would have adapted to the American lifestyle in the way she did, and I doubt still further that she would have made such a lasting impression on those with whom she came into contact. As my tennis partner Mrs. Meech had foreseen, the trip had left me very proud of my famous great-grandmother, and eager to tell her story to the Japanese public.

The time came for me to set off across the Pacific again. My son sat dozing peacefully beside me, catching up on some sleep after four hectic weeks of summer camp. To keep me company, however, I had thoughts of those who had done so much for me over the previous weeks—Mrs. Case, always animated and brimming with curiosity, the chivalrous Alfred Bacon, who never sat down before I did, and Mrs. Bryant, who told me that my visit had encouraged her to take a fresh look at Japan—to name but a few.

The Tragedy of
the Aizu Domain

A SAMURAI DAUGHTER

I was born in 1860. My father, grandfather, all my ancestors for ages past, had been warriors, or, as we used to say, samurai. I might say that I was born in the midst of war, for in the early sixties began the troubles which ended in the War of the Restoration.

"Our feudal prince, the Prince of Aidzu, was one of the last to surrender to the imperial troops in the contest between the shogun and the emperor, or, as he was then called, the mikado. Our prince's castle was at Wakamatsu, and during the last months of the war—when I was eight years old—all the families of the samurai were taken into the castle.

"When I say families, I mean the women and the children of our clan, for all the men were at the front fighting with our prince. Quite near us, to be sure, so that we were in constant communication with them to help them in many ways.

"We women and children were divided into bands of workers, viz.: those who washed and cooked the rice (no light labor, be it known, for Japanese rice is washed, or rather scrubbed, round and round in big buckets until the water becomes white like milk and the palm of the washer is red from the friction), those who did the housework, and those who made the ammunition for the men at the front.

"I was too young to be trusted with the making of cartridges, so the work allotted me was to bring the leaden balls from the storehouses, and after they had been made up into cartridges to carry them back to another storehouse, whence they were sent to the men.

"I must tell you that at this time, when our clan was making its last stand, all the boys above fifteen years of age were with the men at the front, fighting, and there were also a number of boys between twelve and fifteen who made themselves into a regiment and fought against the imperial troops. I think that but few foreigners have heard of the existence of this boy regiment, and I know that it has never been written about.

"When the end of the war came, all the princes of the different clans, with their troops, made peace with the mikado's government, all except this regiment of boys [White Tiger Brigade], who, rather than suffer the humiliation of surrender, committed hara-kiri; that is, killed themselves by opening the abdomen with the short sword or dirk carried by all warriors at that time.

"This blade looks very much like a hunting-knife; it is nine and a half inches long, pointed, and as sharp as a razor. Death by the hara-kiri is horribly painful. The knife is thrust into the left side of the bowels, up to the hilt, and then drawn sharply to the other side, with a slight upward cut at the end.

"Hara-kiri has been and is still considered a most honorable way of passing out of this life. Not only was it the mode of suicide reserved especially for military men, but it is the recognized mode of cleaning off one's moral slate, so to speak, and any real or imaginary blot on one's escutcheon is to this day wiped off by committing hara-kiri.

"I had a sister who at this time was fourteen. Her work was making cartridges—quite too tame an employment according to her ideas, because she wanted to be a mighty warrior.

"One morning she appeared dressed as a boy in all the odd pieces of armor she could find, her long hair cut short and the corners of her pretty little mouth drawn down in true 'mighty warrior' style. She was going to fight, too, and it was only her inborn spirit of obedience which prevented her from running away when my mother refused her consent to her eldest daughter's joining the ranks.

"To return to our life in the castle. The last month of the siege, the imperial troops planted guns on the hills around us, and not a day passed when cannon-balls did not whiz over our heads, dropping into the castle and crashing into the keep itself.

"It was then part of my work to roll them together in piles, out of the way.

"My mother, sister, sister-in-law and I expected death at any minute—that we made up our minds to—but we none of us liked the idea of being mutilated instead of killed outright. So we made our mother promise that if any of us should be mortally wounded she would cut off our heads in true samurai fashion.

"A few days after this, while we were snatching a mouthful of food, a shell fell into the room, and bursting, wounded my sister-in-law in the breast and me in the neck.

My wound was nothing to speak of, and I was up and at work again at the end of the week. It was different with my sister-in-law. We saw that she must die, and a messenger was at once sent to the fighting-line to find my brother and bring him to the castle to bid his wife a last adieu.

"She, poor thing, suffered tortures, and it was pitiful to hear her beg to be put out of her misery.

"'Mother, mother, kill me! Where is your courage? Remember you are the wife of a samurai! Do you forget your promise? In pity kill me quickly!'

"But my mother, poor woman, had been through too much, and her courage failed her when she was called upon to give this supreme proof of love. She simply lacked the strength to keep her promise, so the poor girl suffered agonies, and died a few hours before the arrival of my brother.

"During the last thirty days of the siege, our foe drew his lines so closely about us that our warriors, who up to that time had been guarding the mountain-passes near by, were obliged to take refuge in the castle.

"We were surrounded on every side, but we defended ourselves stoutly and replied so vigorously to the fire of the besiegers that they were obliged to construct another battery over against the southeast corner of the castle, from which they kept up an energetic bombardment.

"We were at the very end of our resources and determined to resort to desperate measures; so on one occasion after the enemy had fired upon us all day without ceasing, our garrison decided to make a night sortie in force, to the east of the castle. At midnight our clan surprised the sleeping camp; the besiegers were defeated and dispersed, with great loss in both killed and wounded, our men retreating in safety to the castle.

"The next morning our adversaries rallied and

bombarded us with shell, creating such havoc that we were absolutely appalled.

"We saw that resistance would be futile, still we could not make up our minds to surrender.

"What do you suppose we did to give our opponents the idea that we were not at all hard pressed, but had plenty of leisure for amusement?

"A lot of us girls were told off to sail kites, a pastime reserved for holidays, when men and boys alike join in the sport, and sail them we did, until our provisions were exhausted and famine forced us to surrender.

"Strange as it may seem, my future husband was one of the attacking force and was wounded during the night assault. Little did I dream that I should be the wife of one of the enemy whose cannon-balls I so carefully rolled into heaps."

("The Marchioness Oyama" by John Dwight, *The Twentieth Century Home*, 1904.)

This story relates the final defeat of the Aizu, a powerful feudal domain, as told by Sutematsu to the American magazine *The Twentieth Century Home* almost ninety years ago. Much has been written about the Aizu War in Japanese, but this is probably the only eyewitness account in English. It is interesting to speculate on what American readers thought of Sutematsu's description of the ritual suicide of the White Tiger Brigade (*Byakkotai*) or of her sister's determination to join in the fight.

The conclusion of the Aizu War ushered in a new era in Japanese history—a drive toward modernization. It is unlikely however that the small daughter of a samurai family, particularly one disgraced by its supposed opposition to the emperor, ever dreamed that she would be sent to a far-off land to spend the greater part of her youth helping to spearhead that drive. Without any conscious intention on her part, Sutematsu's life was to be caught up in the policies of the Meiji government.

THE AIZU CODE

The Aizu Basin is a region of breathtaking scenery, located in the north on the main Japanese island of Honshu. When the swans of Lake Inawashiro have flown north, and the long, bitterly cold winter has come to an end, the fields and mountains are cloaked in green as trees come back to life. Melted snow irrigates fertile land to produce high-quality Aizu rice, used to manufacture the distinctive local brew of sake. The conclusion of the short summer brings a display of eye-catching reds and yellows that stand out in startling contrast to the clear blue skies.

It was here that Sutematsu Yamakawa, known in her early childhood as Sakiko, was born on February 24, 1860. She was the youngest daughter of Hisae Shigekata Yamakawa, a chief retainer of the Aizu domain. Any traces of the Yamakawa family home have long since vanished, and on the site today stands a rather unimaginative collection of local government buildings.

For generations the Yamakawas had been in the service of the Hoshina family, descendants of a lord who had founded the Aizu. Sutematsu's father died a month before she was born, and the little girl was brought up by her grandfather Shigefusa and her mother Toi.

Toi was also the daughter of an Aizu samurai and married Shigekata Yamakawa when she was twenty. She gave birth to twelve children, unfortunately only seven of whom survived. Eager that they be educated, on the long winter evenings she would gather them together and read from various classical works. Coming from a samurai family, Toi was particularly conscious of maintaining the Aizu's samurai code, and no child who acted out of order was spared punishment.

Despite its location in the isolated north of the main Japanese island, the Aizu prided itself on a high standard of education in comparison with other domains. An official school known as the "Nisshinkan" was founded in 1804, which the sons of high-ranking samurai entered at the age of ten. There they were instructed in Confucian doctrines through the original Chinese text and Japanese classics, the Shinto religion, astronomy, arithmetic, and medicine, and also received a thorough grounding in horsemanship, archery, and Judo. The school's facilities were as comprehensive as its curriculum, and included dormitories, study rooms, an observatory, printing shop, library, and even a swimming pool. The Nisshinkan was by far the best institution of its type in the northern region, and counted among its students many who later became leading figures in Japanese education such as Hideo Takamine, principal of the Women's Higher Normal School, Kajinosuke Ibuka, founder of Meiji Gakuin, Sutematsu's brothers Taizo—who became the principal of Tokyo Higher Normal School—and Kenjiro, who became president of the University of Tokyo.

In the last years of the shogunate, it was the Aizu more than any other that most strictly observed its code of conduct. That code—or "Aizu spirit"—devised in 1668, had been respected and upheld for two hundred years by every member of the Aizu, from the most high-ranking samurai to humble foot soldiers and the women and children. It was instilled in the minds of children from an early age: at home, during play, and for the sons of samurai ultimately at the Nisshinkan. Samurai residences were divided into nine separate areas, and the children living in each did almost everything together. The older ones went to school together and studied at home together, while their younger siblings formed play and discussion groups. Within these groups no distinction was made based on family status, and the eldest member was always the leader. To leave the group was forbidden, and whenever the children gathered the leader would remind all present of the importance of following the rules, including obeying and bowing to their elders, telling the truth, not acting cowardly, and not bullying those weaker than themselves.

The group could begin its study games or playing only after everyone had promised to obey these and other rules, and any member who violated one or more of them was judged and punished by his peers. The samurai class of the Aizu were thus subjected to strict discipline from an early age, and its members grew up fiercely proud of their origins.

"Grandma was always a stickler for manners." My father never mentioned Sutematsu without including that comment. No matter how much she loved her grandchildren, it seems Sutematsu did not tolerate misbehavior, attributable, perhaps, to the Aizu code under which she was brought up.

THE ROAD TO WAR

The Aizu's road to tragedy was sealed when in August 1862, Katamori Matsudaira, the lord of Aizu, accepted from the Tokugawa shogun the post of Protector of the Emperor in Kyoto.

Some ten years previously, Commodore Matthew Perry had sailed his squadron of warships into Uraga Bay and demanded that Japan open its doors to trade. Opinions were divided between those who hoped that the nation's long self-imposed isolation was at an end, and those who wished the foreigners would just go away; and between pro-imperial, anti-Tokugawa forces and those who were loyal to the Tokugawa shogun. A heated debate raged across the country, and the 250-year-old institution of the shogunate began to crumble from within. Shimoda Treaty, opening the ports of Shimoda and Hakodate to American vessels, was signed in 1854 by a shogunate government with no experience of diplomacy, with the result that the British, French, Russians, and Dutch struck while the iron was hot and forced their own treaties on Japan shortly thereafter.

Simmering resentment toward the shogunate boiled over into disturbances all over the country, instigated by samurai supporting the restoration of the sovereign rights of the emperor from the Tokugawa government. Some of those men, particularly the lower-ranking samurai of the Satsuma (southern Kyushu island), Choshu, and Tosa domains (western domains of Honshu and Shikoku islands), went too far and only succeeded in alienating would-be supporters by their arrogant conduct. The men of the Satsuma domain, in particular, had harbored generations-old feelings of revenge toward Tokugawa forces since the battle of 1600, when they had suffered defeat and became Tokugawa vassals.

In an attempt to overcome the crisis, the shogunate took a number of steps. An imperial princess was married off to the Tokugawa shogun Iemochi. The shogunate initiated moves to unite with the imperial court, creating a number of new posts, such as that of guardian of the shogun, and chief minister of the government. The position of Protector of the Emperor in Kyoto, in effect that of maintaining security around the imperial court, was delegated, as mentioned before, to the Aizu lord Katamori Matsudaira. Why was the Aizu domain selected?

In 1643 Masayuki Hoshina, the illegitimate son of the second Tokugawa shogun Hidetada, received 230,000 *koku* (one *koku* equalling 5 bushels of rice, or enough to feed a person for a year) of fertile land in the Aizu region from the third Tokugawa shogun Iemitsu and became the founder of the Aizu domain. Thereafter, the Hoshina family descendants were given the name Matsudaira, a name exclusively reserved for all illegitimate offspring of the shogun. From that time on, loyalty to the shogun became a vital part of the samurai-class Aizu creed, and a strict code to be followed by every samurai-class man, woman, and child in the domain. To follow the code was equated with showing respect to the domain's ancestors. This reputation for loyalty, combined with the fact that lords of the domain were buried in Shinto ceremonies (which were associated with the imperial court) rather than the more common Buddhist ceremony, made the Aizu the most obvious candidates for protectors of the throne.

Despite their obvious suitability for the position, however, the Aizu vassals in Edo stationed at the official domain residence declined to take up the position, for fear of being caught up in political wrangling. But pressure from the shogunate not to violate the domain code of loyalty persuaded Katamori as a lord that he was honor-bound to obey the shogun and share the fate of his government.

It is said that Katamori's vassals, who were themselves prepared to die with their lord in any battle over Kyoto, cried bitter tears over Katamori's fate and the Aizu's bad luck in being chosen for such a role. Even they, however, could not have imagined that only a few years later thousands of Aizu samurai and their families would be branded enemies of the throne, and banished to a miserable existence in a remote northern corner of Honshu island.

On December 24, 1862, Katamori, in his new role as Protector of the Emperor in Kyoto, entered the city with a thousand of his armed samurai. The efficiency with which the Aizu security force restored law and order soon earned them the respect of Kyoto citizens, and the seeming courage of the young lord in protecting his emperor even if it meant sacrificing his own life earned Katamori the admiration and affection of Emperor Komei.

The year 1864 brought increased turmoil to the city, and the Aizu security forces were put to good use. As members of the Shinsengumi, a special police force of the shogunate, they killed a number of Choshu and Tosa activists in what became known as the Ikedaya Incident, and joined with Satsuma forces to keep enraged Choshu samurai demanding the overthrow of the shogunate out of Kyoto.

Within two years, however, there was a complete turnaround in the political situation. Satsuma, which had at one time made a secret pact with Aizu, now linked up with Choshu. The Aizu, however, saw their mission to protect Kyoto as one of overriding importance, and lacked the political acumen to see the changes that were taking place around them.

In 1866 the shogun Iemochi died, and soon after Emperor Komei passed away, with the result that the Satsuma's efforts to overthrow the shogunate became increasingly overt. In 1868 at New Year's, when Katamori—by then commander of the Tokugawa government forces—tried to escort the shogun Yoshinobu (who wanted to quell the transpiring coup d'etat to "restore imperial rule") from Osaka Castle to Kyoto, he was obstructed at Toba Fushimi, on the southern outskirts of Kyoto, by an army consisting of Satsuma and Choshu soldiers. On the fourth day of the ensuing battle the rebel army raised the imperial banner in a show of victory, and the Aizu forces were ironically caught in a position of fighting against the "imperial flag." The Satsuma and Choshu conspiracy had worked; from that day onward the Aizu were inadvertently branded as bandits.

Matters were made even worse when Yoshinobu, with whom they had retreated to Osaka Castle, gave up the chance of a possible victory on the battlefield and fled to Edo, taking Katamori and the other generals with him. Once there, in a complete about-face, the shogun made public his allegiance to the throne, despite having promised his generals that their reason for returning to headquarters in Edo was to work on battle strategies.

In February Katamori and his army were ordered to leave Edo, and for the first time in six years returned to the principal domain fortress in Aizu Wakamatsu. There they adopted a low profile and expressed their loyalty to the emperor, petitioning the new government several times to no avail. Two months after their departure imperial forces filled the areas surrounding Aizu, and rumors abounded of a punitive campaign against the domain. At first Katamori had no desire to fight, but realizing that no amount of petitioning would improve the Aizu's situation, he decided he had no choice. He launched a bold attack on Shirakawa castle, thirty miles south of Aizu Wakamatsu, on April 20. The Aizu War had begun.

THE SIEGE

At nine o'clock on the morning of August 23, 1868, those who lived around the Aizu fortress heard through the driving rain the sound of a bell summoning them to refuge within the castle walls.

The previous evening, a preliminary notice had been circulated stating that all samurai and their families were to go to the castle if they heard the fire bell. Most had spent a sleepless night watching the flames already raging from the direction of nearby Lake Inawashiro. No one had expected, however, that in a single night the enemy would advance and penetrate the castle walls with cannon fire even before the warning bell was rung.

Meanwhile, Katamori had been fighting a desperate rearguard action from his base in Takizawaguchi, where he had camped with members of the White Tiger Brigade and two hundred foot soldiers. But the Aizu army was no match for the much larger imperial forces, which consisted of three thousand men of the Satsuma, Tosa, and Sadohara who had managed to get close enough to shell Katamori's base. With the situation rapidly deteriorating, he decided to pull out and retreat to Tsuruga Castle, the main Aizu castle.

The Yamakawa home lay near the northern gate of the castle. Taizo, the eldest son, had left to fight in Tajima, twenty-five miles away, some time before, while the second son, Kenjiro, had left only the previous day to join Katamori's forces at Takizawa on the northern outskirt of Tsuruga Castle. Left behind to take refuge in the castle were Sutematsu's mother, Toi, the remaining four children—including Sutematsu—and Taizo's wife, Tose.

Chaos reigned as people rushed to seek protection within the castle walls. Many panicked and tore back and forth amid the howling wind and torrential rain, slipping and becoming covered in mud. Children screamed as they were cut down by enemy bullets. People were shot as they fled carrying aged parents on their backs. Others died after helping their parents to commit *seppuku* (the correct term for hara-kiri, ceremonial suicide by slitting the belly). Nightmare scenes followed one after the other as the castle was surrounded by imperial forces.

More tragedies were occurring at the homes of the absent samurai. Although they were permitted to take refuge in the castle, many women felt that their presence would hinder their fathers, husbands, and sons in the fighting, and would be a drain on the domain's precious food supply, particularly if the siege were prolonged. They therefore decided to stay where they were, but rather than be humiliated by the enemy forces, chose to commit suicide. All the members of some families ended their lives that way, after dressing themselves in funereal white and enjoying a last drink of sake together. On that first day alone over two hundred people died by their own hand, including the wife of chief retainer Saigo, who killed her small children and then herself. In the Saigo household a total of twenty-one women and children died.

That day also saw the demise of the White Tiger Brigade, as recalled by Sutematsu in her reminiscences for *The Twentieth Century Home*. Nineteen members of the unit, really only boys, had been wandering in a nearby forest since the night before, after the death of their commander. Looking down from a hill above the castle and surrounding village, they saw great clouds of smoke rising from the burning houses, and through the morning mist, they imagined the dim outline of their own castle being bombarded. Exhausted and confused, the boys mistakenly thought that the castle had already been taken, and killed themselves in despair.

By the time the gates were closed, approximately a thousand women, children, and old people had escaped into the castle and were awaiting the arrival of Katamori and his army. The news of the siege soon reached other units stationed on the borders of the Aizu domain, and one after the other they broke through the enemy encirclement and returned to defend the castle.

On the twenty-sixth, Sutematsu's brother Taizo returned to Aizu with about a thousand of his men. Finding the castle completely surrounded and realizing that an attack would involve considerable bloodshed, he devised an ingenious way of getting in.

The Aizu region has a traditional lion dance that is performed at the spring equinox. Every year the local people don lions' heads decorated with black feathers, and bright costumes, then go dancing to the castle accompanied by flutes and drums. Disguised as farmers in festive lion costumes, Taizo and his men succeeded in passing through enemy lines into the castle, while the imperial soldiers looked on unwittingly.

Taizo's ingenuity enabled a combined force of three thousand soldiers to assemble within the castle walls, and the defenders settled in for a protracted siege. Taizo himself was made chief retainer for his remarkable effort, and took overall charge of military operations.

Every one of the defenders, whether soldier, woman, or child, was aware that a fight to the death could ensue, and no doubt the stoicism—inculcated in them from an early age as part of the "Aizu spirit"—helped them to prepare for that possibility.

Katamori's sister-in-law took charge of the women and children inside the castle and oversaw the nursing of wounded, preparation of food, and extinguishing of fires. The samurai wives armed themselves with swords, rolled up their sleeves, and threw themselves into the tasks assigned them. The most dangerous of their chores was throwing wet quilts and clothing onto enemy cannonballs as they landed, to stop them from exploding. It was wounds received while performing this duty that killed Sutematsu's sister-in-law, Tose.

The imperial forces had been confident of a quick victory, but they had underestimated the determination of the Aizu. Inside the castle, however, the ever-decreasing number of defenders were witness to an unrelenting succession of hellish scenes. People were blown away by cannon fire as the enemy kept up a constant bombardment, fires raged day and night, and homes were reduced to smoldering ashes. Food stocks dwindled. The people were surviving on a meager diet of cooked unpolished rice and bean paste.

Ten days after the siege began, on September 8, 1868, the era name changed to Meiji. A new government was officially proclaimed under the Meiji emperor. Dragonflies began to fill the clear autumn skies. The Aizu autumn is short, so the defenders knew that cold weather was not far behind. If they persisted in their defense of the castle the food supply would completely run out, and there were serious shortages of other necessities.

The situation could not have been worse: the castle was surrounded by thirty thousand imperial troops, and the Yonezawa domain, allies of the Aizu, had surrendered on the fourth, leaving them isolated and without support. On the fourteenth, the attackers surrounded the castle on four sides with sixty cannons and began an all-out bombardment. After three days the walls resembled a sieve, but still there was no move to surrender. In defiance, the children were made to fly kites to show the enemy their unfailing morale.

On hearing of the collapse of his allies, however, Katamori decided that surrender was a better option than making his people fight on to certain death, and on September 19 he capitulated to the government.

On September 22 a white flag was raised above the battlements. This flag had been sewn by the women of the Aizu the previous night, who as they performed the task were said to have wept bitter tears over their defeat.

Thus the Aizu War came to an end, exactly a month after the warning bell had sounded, calling the defenders to their castle. A red carpet was laid on the street where the formal surrender took place, and history has it that each of the Aizu warriors took home a small piece of it as a reminder of his clan's bitter defeat. At the ceremony Katamori presented a letter of apology to the government, while the chief retainers submitted a petition asking that their lord and his family be treated mercifully. With this ceremony the curtain closed on the proud two-hundred-year history of the Aizu domain.

THE REFUGEES

Katamori returned to the castle to bid farewell to his vassals. He placed flowers on the graves and in the empty wells in which those who had died during the siege were buried, and as he walked through the devastated town, he was subjected to the jeers and howls of derision of the new government troops. He stopped in Takizawa village, entering Myokokuji temple to repent the Aizu's misguided struggle against imperial forces. The warriors remaining in the castle were sent to Inawashiro near the lake, the wounded to the government army hospital in the village of Aoki, and the noncombatants to Shiokawa village a few miles away from the capital town, along with soldiers who had fought outside the castle walls.

Sutematsu left for Shiokawa with her grandfather, mother, and three sisters. After the month-long siege her hair was full of lice, and her only set of clothing was covered in dirt. During the journey the family stopped over at a temple for a night, and the young Sutematsu was flabbergasted at the sight of white rice, exclaiming, "It's white! It's white, Mother!"   The following morning the Yamakawas arrived in the village of Shiokawa, where they settled down to await news from the government concerning their future.

The family had emerged from the conflict relatively fortunate, the sole casualty being Taizo's wife. Almost miraculously, Taizo and Kenjiro had survived the heavy fighting. The rest of the family were not to enjoy their company for long, however, as the two sons left their mother and sisters soon afterward to pursue their destinies in vastly different careers.

Taizo was to maintain communication links between former Aizu samurai families called to take up residence in Tokyo, the new capital of the Meiji government. He played a vital role in negotiations with the government over the resurrection of the Matsudaira family name and the future of the Aizu samurai.

Kenjiro, meanwhile, who had been a student of exceptional ability during his days at the Nisshinkan, was continuing his studies in the capital under an assumed name to escape exile when the government began recruiting young men to study overseas, with the intention of sending them to work in the new territories of Hokkaido on their return.   Kenjiro applied and was one of the ten chosen to go, despite the fact that he had once fought against government forces.   Deputy Director of the Hokkaido Development Bureau Kiyotaka Kuroda's decision to send the candidate from Aizu was based on his admiration of the domain's courage, and the fact that the Aizu were accustomed to cold conditions and therefore ideally suited for life in Hokkaido. At first Kenjiro was ordered to leave for Russia, but after much protestation he was permitted to change his destination to the United States, and departed from Yokohama on January 1, 1871. Thus it happened that, in an age when very few Japanese even dreamed of going overseas, two members of the same family were to spend years in America as part of the

Meiji government's Hokkaido policy, simply because they had been born into the Aizu.

EXILE IN TONAMI

In November of 1869 the Meiji government permitted the revival of the Matsudaira name with Katamori's heir Kataharu, who was a year old at the time. That concession provided the Aizu warriors in exile—who since the war had been unsure of their status and were living in limbo—with a faint glimmer of hope. They were granted land by the government, but what they received was a bleak thirty thousand koku tract of wasteland in the Mutsu region of northern Honshu island, a far cry from the 230,000 koku of fertile land they had owned before the war. Nevertheless, the Aizu chose to leave their ancestral homeland and head north: partly as a gesture of conciliation toward the new government, and partly because, after losing everything in the war, the idea of bringing new lands in the boundless north under cultivation was an attractive one and seemed to offer the better chance for a revival of Aizu fortunes.

The new domain was known as Tonami, and was located in present-day Aomori and Iwate Prefectures. Two other domains split the new Aizu territory in half. It was under this unusual set of circumstances that the Aizu began their new life.

From the spring of 1870 the Aizu samurai exiled in Tokyo, Inawashiro, and Echigo (present-day Niigata) began to head north to Tonami with their families. In all, seventeen thousand people made the journey, some traveling across country, others going by sea. Sutematsu left Aizu Wakamatsu with her mother, sisters, and the other members led by Taizo.

With little more than the clothes on their backs, the party traveled on foot to Tsugawa, from which they sailed down the Aga River to Niigata, arriving four days later. At Niigata they boarded the American paddlesteamer *Yancy*, which had been chartered by the Japanese government for the purpose of transporting the emigrants.

At first the party found plenty to interest them on board ship: for most it was their first view of the sea, and they wandered around on deck in excitement, cautiously nibbling the biscuits the American seamen had given them. Once the novelty of an ocean voyage began to wear off, though, they were left with the daunting prospect of settling in an unknown land, with all the problems that entailed, and spent the remainder of the trip lying seasick and sleepless in their quarters.

When the *Yancy* docked at the port of Nobeji in Mutsu Bay on June 21, the Yamakawas' first stop was at the new domain government office. Sutematsu's brother Taizo was already assigned as head of the domain council, governing for the child-lord Kataharu, and the fate of seventeen thousand people rested squarely on his shoulders.

The settlers soon found themselves in the midst of severe winter conditions and a food shortage. Although they had been given thirty thousand koku, the land was covered in snow for half the year and only seven thousand of it could be cultivated, an area not nearly adequate for the needs of four thousand households. Having come to Tonami in search of self-sufficiency, the people had only two hundred *mon*—just barely enough with which to buy food, clothing, and accommodation—and a small ration of rice per day.

To fend off starvation they ate mountain plants, soybeans that in better times would have been used for horse feed, rice porridge mixed with the roots of seaweed, even the occasional dog. The promised land was not living up to even the settlers' modest expectations. Deaths from malnutrition followed one after the other, with the people too poor to provide even a simple funeral for their loved ones. To the survivors it seemed that they too had died and descended into some horrible hell.

The Aizu were not unused to harsh winters, but they were

accustomed to spending them in proper houses: their accommodation in Tonami amounted to little more than huts, with not even tatami matting on the floor. The north wind was so icy that when it blew through the settlers' homes, it caused the porridge in the grate to freeze.

Despite living under such conditions, the settlers retained their Aizu spirit. One of their compatriots writes in the book *Aru Meijijin no kiroku* (*One Man's Memories during Meiji*):

> If we, the beggar warriors of Aizu, starve to death up here, we'll be the laughingstock of even the lowest samurai class of the Satsuma and Choshu. We must survive until the day when we can take our revenge for the insults we've endured. The battle is far from over.

A GLIMPSE OF THE WEST

Despite the eldest Yamakawa son acting as domain leader, the family was poorer than any other, perhaps due to his determination to set a good example to the other settlers. Sutematsu was eleven years old by that time, and working hard for the family. Every day she and her sisters would walk off to the fields with buckets of nightsoil to spread, and go into the rivers in search of fish and shellfish to supplement their meager diet.

Aware that he was unable to provide enough food for his growing sisters, Taizo, who had now adopted the name Hiroshi, decided to send the youngest, Sutematsu, to Hakodate in Hokkaido, after discussing the idea with his mother. Life there could only be better than the hand-to-mouth existence at Tonami.

Traditionally, the Aizu had had a long association with the town of Hakodate. Toward the end of the Edo period the domain had established a branch office in Hakodate to administer its lands on the coast, and had also fought government forces there after the Aizu War, holing up in a castle in the town in a last-ditch effort to defeat the Meiji government.

Unfortunately, there is no record of where Sutematsu was placed, but one possibility is that she was entrusted to a foreign missionary's family: in the Vassar College archives there is a record of her commenting to a classmate that she had "left home and lived with a French family in Hakodate." Since its opening to the outside world in 1854, the port of Hakodate had become a lively town where foreign ships stopped to fuel, and traders came to buy up large quantities of Hokkaido's abundant marine products. Nine countries had established consulates there by the time of the Restoration, with beautiful Western-style homes for their staff. In short, the town had a cosmopolitan air, and the locals had long since ceased to find their foreign visitors unusual. To Sutematsu, whose main concern during her time in Tonami had been finding enough to eat, it was as if she had arrived in another country. Although her stay in Hakodate was relatively short—only six months—it allowed her a glimpse—and a prelude—of the real West to come.

The Iwakura Mission

THE RECRUITMENT

𝓕n May 1869 the last resistance to the new government was quelled when the shogun's deputy naval commander and his followers surrendered after a showdown in Hakodate. The Meiji Restoration was finally achieved in substance as well as name. The northern island of Ezo was renamed Hokkaido that same year and the Development Bureau shifted from Tokyo to Hakodate. A budget of ten million yen, a considerable sum for the time, was allocated for the settlement and development of Hokkaido over a ten-year period.

May of the following year brought a new appointee to the post of deputy minister for the bureau: Kiyotaka Kuroda of Satsuma. The post was a reward to Kuroda for his victory in the Battle of Hakodate. In Kuroda's opinion, a "frontier spirit" had to be fostered if Hokkaido was to be opened up successfully, and the easiest way to nurture such a spirit was to learn from the Americans, who had set an example with the settling of their western territories. Kuroda set off to find out in more detail for himself the kind of frontier work being carried out in the States, at the same time as Sutematsu's brother Kenjiro was leaving for his period of study there. Speaking with President Grant, Kuroda informed him of the situation in Hokkaido and requested that skilled American experts be sent to aid with the region's development.

Kuroda was assisted during his stay in Washington by the Japanese representative, Arinori Mori, who at the time was barely twenty-five years old. Mori was of the same Satsuma origins as Kuroda and had been sent to London at the age of seventeen by his lord, then to America, where he had worked on a Quaker farm while continuing his studies. Thus, despite his youth, Mori was well-versed in the culture and customs of Western countries.

As a diplomat, Mori had given considerable thought while in Washington to the road that the new Japan should take toward modernization. The key to joining the club of modern nations, he decided, was education, and he wrote letters to prominent American politicians and intellectuals, canvassing their opinions on the subject. Of particular interest is a letter addressed to Yale professor of linguistics William Whitney, father of Marian Whitney, a young woman who later became one of Sutematsu's closest friends. In it Mori expresses the opinion that "Japanese is a difficult language which cannot be taught or learnt without *kanji* [Chinese characters]. Therefore to pursue all the knowledge the West has to offer us we would perhaps be better to discard Japanese and use only English for the purpose of learning." The professor disagreed and replied, "A nation should not seek to advance its own culture using another nation's language." Mori's letter is a good example of the urgency with which Japan's leaders desired acceptance by the West during the early Meiji period, and shows their willingness to go to extremes to achieve that aim.

Kiyotaka Kuroda was of a like mind. What had surprised him

most about the United States were the American women. Compared with those at home they were outgoing and seemed much happier. They freely exchanged views with men, and many did the same work as males. Kuroda wondered in what sort of environment these women were brought up, and discussed them often with Mori. The two men came to the conclusion that educating females in the same manner as males was the key to speeding up Japan's drive toward modernization, and that the idea should be put into practice by the Hokkaido Development Bureau as soon as possible.

On his return to Japan Kuroda submitted a report to the government, which suggested that sending young girls to America to study would be far more effective in the long term than sending uneducated males to work on development projects in Hokkaido. This recommendation was based on the dubious premise that intelligent women would become intelligent mothers, and intelligent mothers must give birth to children equally as endowed with brains, who in turn would make ideal settlers. The Bureau would of course pay all the girls' costs overseas. Tomomi Iwakura, a court noble who at the time was recruiting male students to accompany his overseas mission, was in total agreement with Kuroda and quickly resolved to take some female students along as well.

For all the long hours that two leading figures in the Meiji government had spent debating the idea in the United States, the practicalities of the scheme were arranged in a great hurry. The plan lacked foresight and long-term planning, remaining very much a vehicle for Kuroda's pet theory—not a comprehensive government program as it should have been. Another problem was that while at first glance it seemed progressive in terms of the advancement of women, it was in fact nothing of the kind. Those who formulated it closed their eyes to the injustices Japanese women had suffered for centuries under the feudal system. They never deviated from their view that men were the rightful leaders of society, and that the main function of women was producing children.

Although one could perhaps expect no different from a society that was far from ready to accept equality between the sexes, it is still a great shame that only one group of Japanese females was ever dispatched overseas during the Meiji Period.

On gaining approval in October 1871, Kuroda began recruiting young girls to travel with the Iwakura Mission to the United States. The period of stay was to be ten years, and travel costs, school fees, and living costs were to be provided from public funds, along with eight hundred dollars spending money per annum. A dollar was equivalent to approximately one yen. Five yen at the time bought a couple of square yards of land on the Ginza in the heart of Tokyo's premier shopping district, so eight hundred dollars was an incredible amount for a small girl to receive as pocket money. Despite this, there was not one applicant: hardly surprising in an age when girls were considered useful for housework and child-minding, until around the age of fifteen when they were married off. Like their counterparts of the lower classes, the daughters of samurai families were also brought up to be good wives and mothers, and in addition were trained in traditional feminine accomplishments such as flower-arranging and tea ceremony before being sent off to their husband's household. Spending ten years overseas would leave a girl too old to marry when she returned, quite apart from the fact that no parents in their right mind would send their daughter to live in a barbaric country like America, where it was said the people ate unspeakable parts of cattle and pigs, and drank vast quantities of a bright red liquid which some suspected to be blood.

As the departure date of the Iwakura Mission loomed, the Hokkaido Development Bureau launched a second, desperate, recruitment drive, to which the following five girls finally answered:

Ryoko Yoshimasu, fourteen, of Tokyo
Teiko Ueda, fourteen, of Niigata
Sutematsu Yamakawa, eleven, of Aomori
Shigeko Nagai, eight, of Shizuoka
Umeko Tsuda, six, of Tokyo

All the girls were the daughters of samurai families. Kiyotaka Kuroda, who saw his scheme as the key to Japan's future success, was extremely disappointed with the lack of response. Realizing that five women were hardly adequate to raise the future settlers of Hokkaido, he decided to begin educating them at home instead, and in September of the following year founded a girls' school in Tokyo with the same aim as his original scheme: to produce intelligent mothers. The school, however, was moved to Sapporo in Hokkaido after three years, its curriculum changed from one geared to the general education of women to one of more specialized subjects connected directly with development projects. After a further year it was judged too physically demanding for females and closed down.

Not even twenty years had passed since Commodore Perry first appeared in Uraga Bay and forced the Japanese to open their ports, and an even shorter length of time had elapsed since the movement to expel all foreigners had finally died down. Under such circumstances, what kind of parents could bring themselves to send their young daughter to America for a long stay?

The fathers of the two older girls worked in the foreign ministry, and were relatively knowledgeable about the West. Shigeko Nagai's father had been overseas toward the end of the Edo period, traveling with his son to Europe. They went as members of a Tokugawa government mission in 1863. Umeko Tsuda's father had studied under the Dutch in Japan for many years, had learned English, and had been employed by the shogunate as an interpreter, traveling to the United States at one point to facilitate the purchase of warships for the Japanese navy. Sutematsu's brother Kenjiro was of course already in America studying. Her eldest brother, Hiroshi, had accompanied the shogunate's foreign minister to Russia in 1867 for the signing of a border agreement with that country, then had gone on to Europe for an extensive tour. Apart from their all having some "foreign connection," the five girls had something else in common: all were members of domains that had served the defeated shogunate government. Since the Restoration, their fathers and brothers had been relegated to the position of low-level functionaries with little hope of advancement in a new Meiji government controlled by Satsuma and Choshu men. The time would come soon, the men of the defeated domains reasoned, when Japan would need the knowledge and the technology that they themselves had seen firsthand overseas, and equipping their own daughters with that knowledge by sending them to America was as good a revenge as any.

The inspiration behind sending Sutematsu is even clearer. One of the family precepts of the Aizu domain was that no woman or girl could exchange words with a male once outside the home. Turning this strict rule to their advantage, the female Aizu members were encouraged early on to compete with the boys by developing strength of character and excelling in their studies. The industriousness displayed by the women and young girls during the Aizu War represented a striking achievement unprecedented in Japanese history. Eight-year-old Sutematsu, too, had made her contribution during the dramatic siege in the castle, and was never to forget the nobility of the Aizu spirit.

When the Yamakawas heard of the recruitment, they believed that a stouthearted and sagacious Sutematsu, having persevered through the cruel realities of war, would be able to weather the hardships of living abroad and equal any boy in the mastering of academic studies. If she could live up to the government sponsorship and serve the country, then there would surely come a day when the Aizu name—ironically equated with "enemy of the throne" because of the strict Aizu moral code—would be cleared.

A NEW NAME AND DESTINATION

Just when Sutematsu had finally become accustomed to her new life in Hakodate, brother Hiroshi arrived with some startling news. It was October 1871.

"You're leaving for Tokyo straightaway," he informed her. "Next month you'll go to a place called America, where you'll live and study for ten years as a government student."

Although we have no clue about how Sutematsu really felt, undoubtedly she understood that there was no question of refusing her brother's directive. We can imagine that she might have felt pride in going abroad to study for the sake of her country, but had no concept of the length of ten years.

Leaving Hakodate in mid-October, Sutematsu stopped in Tanabu to bid farewell to her mother and sisters. It was there that Sutematsu's mother changed her beloved daughter's name from Sakiko to Sutematsu, to symbolize her sorrow at having to send the girl to a far-off country. "Sute" means "to discard, abandon" and "matsu" means "to wait," although in Sutematsu's name "matsu" is read using the character for "pine tree," a symbol of long life. Thus Mrs. Yamakawa felt that she was in effect abandoning her daughter to whatever fate awaited her in America, but was determined at the same time to wait, indefinitely, for her return.

With little time for long goodbyes, Sutematsu left her family and hurried to Tokyo, where she and the other four girls immediately began preparations for the journey. Together they attended functions at the Development Bureau and Ministry of Education, and shopped for clothes and other essentials, becoming firm friends in the process. The older girls took special care of Sutematsu because she had no relations in Tokyo, and Sutematsu in turn was delighted to have gained two younger sisters in Umeko and Shigeko. The girls had little time to have Western-style clothes or shoes made, but they did manage to buy new kimonos with money the government provided.

A few days before their departure, they paid their respects to the empress. Each received some cakes, a length of red silk, and instructions to study "day and night" and become role models for future Japanese women when they returned. After the girls left the imperial palace and had a commemorative photograph taken, they were more conscious than ever of the importance of the journey they were about to undertake.

DEPARTURE

A photograph taken of the leaders of the Iwakura Mission just prior to their departure for Europe and the United States shows Ambassador Tomomi Iwakura in traditional Japanese formal dress, befitting his position as head of the mission. Incongruous with this attire he wore a pair of black leather shoes. The others— Councilor Takayoshi Kido, Minister of Finance Toshimichi Okubo, Assistant Minister of Public Works Hirobumi Ito, and Assistant Minister of Foreign Affairs Naoyoshi Yamaguchi—are clasping top hats and appear ill-at-ease in their poorly fitting wrinkled suits. Neither Iwakura's odd combination of Japanese and Western attire nor his fellow delegates' attempts at modern dress could be seen as stylish by any stretch of the imagination. Rather they reflect the new Meiji government's desperate eagerness to be accepted by Western society.

Only a month and a half elapsed between the organization of the Iwakura Mission and its departure. It was a time of great political upheaval. Samurai all over the country were fiercely resisting the reforms put into place in July 1871, whose aims were to do away with the old feudal domains and redistribute the samurai estates and wealth under a prefectural system with a strong central government. Matters were further complicated by the constant infighting between various factions within the government itself. It was imperative, therefore, that Japan's new leaders obtain knowledge of the West as quickly as possible, and use that knowledge to stabilize the political situation and set the nation on a course of modernization.

The revision, scheduled to take place the following year, of the "unequal" treaties signed between the last shogun and several Western nations was another urgent issue for the new government. Before any revision of those treaties could be carried out, Japanese laws first had to be brought into line with international law, a task that could by no means be completed in only one or two years. The mission's members were charged with negotiating an extension of the treaty expiry dates with their American and European counterparts.

The group entrusted with this crucial task consisted of approximately fifty men, all talented members of the new government and predominantly from the Satsuma and Choshu domains. Their specialist abilities encompassed a wide range of fields: politics, economics, finance, education, and the military. The average age of the group was a startling thirty years, as the Meiji government believed that young adaptable heads could best absorb knowledge from the West.

Fifty-nine young students joined the official delegation. Many of them went on to play leading roles in the construction of the modern Japanese state: Nobuaki Makino became minister of education and later foreign affairs, Chomin Nakae made his name in the democratic movement, Takuma Dan headed the Mitsui group of companies, and Kentaro Kaneko drafted the Japanese Imperial Constitution.

Checking on those students already studying overseas at government expense was yet another task of the delegation. In 1872, Charles Lanman, secretary for the Japanese Legation in Washington, stated in his book *The Japanese in America* that approximately five hundred Japanese nationals had already visited the United States by that year, and two hundred were currently in the country. Even assuming his estimates to be high, they still reveal that by the early years of the Meiji period a surprisingly large number of Japanese had crossed the Pacific in search of new horizons. The more progressive lords of Satsuma, Kumamoto, and Fukui domains had in fact been sending their most promising young men overseas since the later years of the feudal period, smuggling them out at a time when such travel was strictly prohibited.

Students sponsored by the new government were given allowances of seven hundred to one thousand dollars per annum, a considerable sum for the time. The lucky few had been chosen by the various ministries for any number of reasons, and the selection process was not always particularly fair. Inevitably there were those who had neither natural ability nor much inclination to study and who preferred to squander their allowances, causing the government a great deal of anxiety. The Iwakura Mission was responsible for identifying those wasters of public funds and sending them back to Japan.

Sutematsu's brother Kenjiro was studying physics at the Sheffield Scientific School at Yale in 1871, and was one of those ordered to return home. Determined to continue his studies, however, he managed to receive financial assistance from a classmate's rich aunt, on the condition that he promise to spend his life in the service of his country when he graduated. Kenjiro succeeded in becoming the first Japanese to graduate from Yale University.

December 23, 1871, dawned a clear day, the frost on the ground sparkling under sunlight that was unusually strong for the time of year. The mail ship *America* made an impressive sight anchored in Yokohama Bay, with the flags of Japan and the United States fluttering from her mast. Friends and relatives of the official delegation and accompanying students had gathered to see the party off, as had a large crowd of people hoping to catch a glimpse of the government bigwigs. The members themselves had already spent several days in Yokohama indulging in a last bout of drinking and celebration. The festivities had a slightly desperate air about them, as if the revelers were afraid they would never set foot on their home soil again. The comic result was that many of those gathered at the wharf that day appeared tired even before their journey had commenced.

The attention of the onlookers was particularly drawn to the group of five female students setting off in a small boat for the *America*, accompanied by the wife of the United States minister De Long. With their hair arranged in simple styles appropriate to their youth, and dressed in kimonos with draping sleeves, the girls' appearances caused a stir among those on the wharf—some of the spectators whispered that the girls' mothers must be very hard-hearted to send their daughters off to a foreign land at such a young age.

Small steamships and sailing boats ferried to and from the vessel until the last of the almost one hundred and twenty participants in the mission were on board the *America*. Nineteen cannon shots were fired from the port in a farewell salute to them, then one more went off for the minister and his wife, who were themselves returning to the United States.

At noon the twenty-first cannon shot signaled the group's departure, and the forty-five-hundred-ton steamer began to move slowly out of the bay, propelled by the huge wheel at its stern. The crews of foreign warships anchored in the harbor lined up on the decks of their vessels, bidding farewell to the travelers.

Slipping out of the Uraga Channel, the ship headed toward the open sea. Those on board were treated to the breathtaking sight of Mt. Fuji and the nearby mountains of Hakone, covered in snow and bathed in the glow of the setting sun. They stayed on deck until the scene was no longer visible, watching with mixed emotions and wondering when they would be able to see it again.

The voyage to San Francisco was a monotonous one, with not even an island to provide some relief, and the occasional visit of a wandering albatross was greeted with great delight. One hundred and twenty people living in close quarters and seeing each other day in, day out is no recipe for harmony, and it is hardly surprising that there was friction among the participants in the mission. The mixture, like a tinderbox, included upstarts from the Satsuma and

Choshu domains as well as former Tokugawa loyalists, who resented many of the changes brought about by the former in the new regime. Some of those from the old Tokugawa regime who had lived overseas before were only too willing to show off their knowledge of Western customs at every opportunity, and relieved their own stress and boredom by poking fun at the upstart officials—men who had never left Japan's shores. Consequently not a day of the voyage went by without an argument of some kind.

On one occasion Yoshimoto Hiraga, a legal official well versed in foreign customs, tried to teach the party the correct way to eat Western food, having noticed that their table manners left much to be desired. With the help of some Westerners on board he compiled a list of rules for mealtimes. Hiraga's advice was not well received by the assistants to the official delegation, most of whom clung stubbornly to their samurai ways. They responded by putting on the worst display they could: slurping their soup, stabbing their steaks and gnawing on them without bothering to cut them up first, and ordering the servants around in a loud and offensive manner. It seemed life on board the *America* was a microcosm of Japan after the Meiji Restoration.

Sutematsu herself was involved in another incident that took place during the voyage. One day she ran to Okubo, shaking with anger, and reported that a young official of the Justice Ministry, allegedly drunk, had pulled the sleeve of one of the older girls, Ryoko Yoshimasu, on her way to the toilet. Not only was the official's action considered an affront, the event was tantamount to a scandal, especially since it involved the daughters of former samurai. The bored members of the mission seized upon the incident as a way of relieving the tedium of the trip and called for a mock trial to be held, despite the opposition of the minister of justice, who claimed that it would only serve to embarrass one of his assistants, not to mention the entire delegation. Hirobumi Ito, who had been chosen to act as the judge, was enthusiastic about the idea. Believing that the trial would provide an excellent opportunity for

those on the mission to become familiar with Western legal proce-
dures, he conducted it in the same manner as those he had
observed in London. The outcome, however, was obvious from
the beginning, and the whole affair was intensely embarrassing for
the young people involved.

This incident illustrates the determination of the elite members
of the Meiji government to adopt Western methods as rapidly as
possible, even at the cost of demoralizing ordinary citizens.

THE WELCOME

Sailing cautiously toward the Golden Gate Bridge through one
of the thick fogs peculiar to the Bay, at long last the *America* arrived
in San Francisco. It was ten o'clock on the morning of January 15,
1872. The party had in fact arrived a day earlier than scheduled,
taking the mayor and his welcoming committee—who had been
preparing for some months—by surprise. It was all they could do
to arrange a fifteen-gun salute from the fortresses of Alcatraz and
Fort Point, and they hurriedly sent the American consul of Japan,
Brooks, to the dock, accompanied by a few federal officials.

After a brief welcoming ceremony, the guests were escorted to
carriages provided by the city and taken to the Grand Hotel on
Montgomery Street. The party turned out to be much larger than
city officials had been informed; it would be forty-five of the students were placed in the Occidental Hotel, and the remaining ten
stayed at The Lick House.

Since no formal ceremonies had been arranged for that day, the
group members checked in at their hotels to unpack and rest. But
there were so many new things to see and experience. Getting to
one's room involved climbing into a kind of box suspended by a
rope, and being dangled in midair. Sleeping was impossible because
there were springs in the mattress that made the body go up and
down. Scalding hot water came out of the bath taps, and disposing
of toilet waste involved pulling a rope to make water stream out.
Hotel staff could be summoned using an electric wire. The rooms

were filled with beautiful mirrors, clocks, desks, chairs, and fire-places: for the Japanese there was nowhere to relax. Venturing out into the lobby they saw immaculately dressed gentlemen strolling arm-in-arm with women, and opening doors for them as if it were the most natural thing in the world. Hailing from a culture where women were still very much second-class citizens, the Japanese men were amazed, and quite repulsed by the sight of males acting like servants, as they saw it.

The residents of the host city were every bit as curious about their guests as their guests were about them, and the San Francisco papers devoted considerable space every day to the people from the land of the "Mikado" and their activities. The *San Francisco Examiner*, for example, described Tomomi Iwakura as follows in its January 15 issue: "He carried two swords in a sash around his waist and the indispensable fan in his hand. Apparently, he is about sixty years of age and anything but prepossessing in appearance."

The unfortunate Iwakura was in fact a sprightly forty-eight at the time. The other men were described in rather unflattering terms, albeit in a lighthearted vein, as "small sized men and from general appearance we do not think any of our San Francisco belles will go wild after them."

By far the most popular members of the party were Sutematsu and her four companions.

Accompanied by the wife of Minister De Long, the women are five in number, and we are informed are all daughters of princes in their kingdom. Unlike their male companions, the princesses are rather comely and attractive in appearance. Their dresses differ little from the costumes worn by the Chinesemen in this city, with the exception that they are very rich and expensive. These five princesses are the first females of noble birth that have ever left their country. . . . They are on their way to Vassar Female Seminary at Poughkeepsie, New York, where they intend to study the manners and customs of American life and society and then elevate the standard of Japanese ladies. This is the first step and should it turn out favorably to their friends, a large number of women will be sent here next year.

(*San Francisco Examiner,* January 15, 1872)

The *Daily Morning Call* of January 17 states:

We are informed [that the girls] will remain secluded until by the art of the American dressmaker and the cunning of the American milliner, they have been transformed from picturesque Oriental belles to rather plain-looking Occidental damsels.

The girls' popularity was such that if they left the hotel a crowd would gather, and curious onlookers would try to touch their kimonos. For a while they confined themselves to the hotel, even taking their meals in their rooms.

The welcome the town of San Francisco gave to the Iwakura Mission was so enthusiastic as to be almost overwhelming. From the morning of the seventeenth the mayor and his welcoming committee, army and navy officers, and consuls from several nations paid calls on Iwakura and his four deputies. The Japanese delegation bowed to and shook hands with each visitor and listened carefully as Consul Brooks and an interpreter relayed their messages. Unused to this kind of meeting, they were exhausted before the morning was out.

On the evening of the formal welcoming ceremony, a crowd struggling to catch a glimpse of the ceremony rendered the street in front of the Grand Hotel impassable. At ten o'clock sharp the band began to play, and Iwakura and his deputies took their seats next to Minister De Long for a program of music that included Wagner, Strauss, and Verdi. When the concert had ended Iwakura and De Long proceeded to the balcony, prompting a great cheer from the crowd. After the noise had died down, Iwakura took out a scroll, later described as "about a yard and a half long, and eighteen inches wide," and began to read his speech in a deep clear voice. On finishing, he bowed deeply to the crowd, sparking another enthusiastic round of applause "better than the greatest orator in America could ever hope for."

A summary of Iwakura's speech was translated by De Long:

> It is now a recognized fact in Japan that, since the conclusion of the treaty between the United States and our country, our prosperity has greatly increased with our new commercial intercourse. Our advancement in the arts and sciences of Western nations are now considered of substantial benefit to our nation and we desire that with every increase of national intercourse there shall be an increase of international friendship. With a view of hastening these results and further facilitating the instruction of our people in the civilization of Western nations, his majesty the Tenno has commissioned us to visit all the countries having treaties with Japan in the capacity of Ambassador Plenipotentiary first visiting your country. The warmth of your reception is an unquestionable proof to us that the friendship of Americans is indeed real, and I assure you that it will remain in the hearts of our people. Your expression of kind feeling when announced to HIM will be made known throughout Japan and assist in further cementing a mutual friendship between our respective countries.
> (*Daily Morning Call*, January 17, 1872)

Wild applause also followed De Long's translation, along with calls for the minister himself to make a speech. He was only too happy to respond.

The consummate politician, De Long had traveled from New York to California to join the gold rush in his younger days, and using his natural talents as a speaker, had got himself elected to the state legislature, then to the Senate. De Long had little formal education, nor any experience as a diplomat, but had just returned from two years in Japan as the fourth American minister to that country.

> This much I will say, however. You must not confound these Japanese with Chinese. [cheers] . . . I can say to you to-night, in all truth that instead of it being an over-populated country, ready to pour forth an emigration, that within five years they will be needing and asking for white labor to develop their mines and their industries, while the Chinese are a subjugated race, with all their energies crushed out of them. The Japanese have never known a master. They are native gentlemen, with all the courage belonging to true nobility. While China is forging her chains and enveloping herself in darkness, Japan, by this Embassy, is striking down the barriers, and introducing on her soil the civilization and enterprises of the Western Nations. It is a duty you owe and are well performing, to receive this Embassy as you are, and you are forming a friendship which would be of lasting and permanent value, and whose effects you will feel in the contingency of a war with China.
> (*Daily Morning Call*, January 17, 1872)

Welcome ceremonies over, the members of the delegation launched themselves into the business of their visit the following day, with the complete cooperation of the municipal authorities.

> The Embassy at present visiting us is composed of men who are shrewd and intelligent, men who are quick to comprehend and slow to forget, and the impressions they receive here being daily recorded in journals for future reference, it should be our aim to show them everything worth seeing in the city.
> (*Daily Evening Bulletin*, January 18, 1872)

The party split up into special interest groups and toured steel plants, shipbuilding yards, textile factories, the city gas company, the courthouse, and several schools. Everywhere they went the Japanese visitors were praised for the speed at which they absorbed all they saw. As the *Evening Bulletin* reporter noted, Kunitake Kume accompanied Iwakura at all times, recording in great detail not only the movements of the delegation but American history, the geography, and anything he saw or heard. Kume's report was eventually published in Japan in 1878, entitled *Tokumei zenken taishi: Beio Kairan Jikki* (The official record of the Iwakura Mission).

The five female students continued to be extremely popular with the press, which described them in the most glowing terms. One evening, Ryoko and Teiko were taken to the theater for the first time in their lives, then on to a ball at the governor's residence. When asked whether they enjoyed the evening one of the girls is quoted as replying, ". . . I did not know there was such a world as this."

Most of what was written about the girls was of this nature, but one article stands out from the others: a welcome message from the chairwoman of the California State Central Women's Suffrage Committee, Elizabeth Schenk.

> In the name of the women of America, the representatives of the State Central Committee of California welcome to our country the women of the Japanese Embassy. We congratulate you on your safe arrival and truly hope your sojourn among us may prove both pleasant and profitable.
>
> We recognize in this visit of the Embassy . . . the forming and strengthening of social ties which make of all nations one family.
>
> The women of Japan and America have, we feel, great reason for encouragement in view of the marked change in both countries in favor of enlarging the educational advan-

tages of women. Your visit to this country has an especial significance to those women of America who have been and are
laboring for the rights and privileges belonging to a broader
field of action than has before been open to them; and they
rejoice that this movement is simultaneous in Japan and other
enlightened nations, marking, as it does, a new era in the history of the world.

An inspiring and optimistic message from a pioneer of the
American women's movement. It is doubtful, however, that Mrs.
Schenk knew the real reason for the girls' trip to America, which
was of course to train them to become intelligent mothers who
would raise promising children, an idea about as far removed from
that of advancing women's rights as could possibly be.

BREAKDOWN IN TREATY NEGOTIATIONS

The year 1872 saw America's heaviest snowfalls in forty years.
Enough snow had fallen in the Rockies to cut off rail communication. After being forced to stay in San Francisco five days longer
than scheduled, on January 31 the Japanese delegates left to begin
their rail journey across the United States. After the warm welcome they had received in San Francisco, Ambassador Iwakura was
confident of success in the forthcoming treaty negotiations in
Washington. By the time he and the rest of the party departed
from San Francisco, they had lost the nervousness they had felt on
leaving Japan.

Snowfalls were still blocking the track in parts, but with the aid
of a snowplow the train managed to crawl into Ogden, Utah. It
went no further, however, and the delegation found itself stuck in
Salt Lake City for an unexpectedly long period, waiting for the
weather to clear. Touring factories, schools, and Mormon churches, the members used the time wisely until February 22, when they
were finally able to depart. After three days traversing the Great
Plains the train crossed the Missouri River and arrived in Chicago.

Traveling across the United States by train, the leaders of the new Japan were impressed with the power of their host country. Despite Japan's far longer history as a nation, it seemed far behind America in every respect. The Americans were religious, and also devoted their energies to a general education for everyone. On the other hand, the Japanese received only a rudimentary education; if they not focused on the accumulation of wealth, they were so poor that they lived from one day to another without knowing where their next meal would come from. Iwakura and his deputies realized that the prosperity of a nation was not dependent on its area or population, but on the quality of its people and their education.

On February 29 the delegation arrived in Washington to find that city also blanketed in snow. It had taken almost a month to cross the continent, and it had taken an incredible two months to get from Yokohama to their final destination—the negotiating table in Washington.

Arinori Mori took Iwakura and his four deputies to the Arlington Hotel, where, forgoing all the official ceremonies, they rested several days in preparation for an audience with President Grant.

They left for the White House just after noon on March 4, wearing traditional Japanese court dress. Their meeting with the President was later described as follows by *Frank Leslie's Illustrated Newspaper*, a popular publication of the time:

> President Grant, with his cabinet on his left, and quite an army of bureau officials on the right, took position of the south end of the famous East Room, the party forming a semi-circular line. The five Ambassadors appeared in front of the Executive Mansion shortly after twelve o'clock, and were accompanied by their four first secretaries and by the senior second secretary, also by the Charge-d'Affaires of Japan in Washington; but no other Japanese were present at any part of the ceremony. The Ambassadors and secretaries were in

Japanese court costume, but Mr. Mori was in American party dress. The underdress of Iwakura and associates was in some cases of purple and in others of dark blue silk . . . [they wore] skull-caps, surmounted by high combs, to which were attached pieces of steel-colored wire gauze, over two feet in length, projecting several inches above the head, and then curving downward. They also wore jeweled swords, carried, it was noticed, on the left side, instead of in front, and no more than one sword apiece. The principals wore American gaiter boots and the secretaries Japanese silk shoes.
(*Frank Leslie's Illustrated Newspaper*, March 23, 1872)

Iwakura presented an official message of greeting from the emperor then made a short speech of his own, to which the President replied, "I am gratified that this country and that my administration will be distinguished in history as the first . . . to establish diplomatic and commercial intercourse. The objects which you say have given rise to your mission do honor to the intelligence and wisdom of your sovereign, and reflect credit on you in having been chosen as the instruments for carrying them into effect. . . . It will be a pleasure to us to enter upon international questions in which you say you are authorized to engage. . . ."

On March 11, treaty revision negotiations finally began between the Japanese delegation and Secretary of State Fish. The visitors, reassured by the enthusiastic welcomes they had received all over America, were confident that talks would go smoothly. But it was not to be. The American negotiators requested a letter of authority from the emperor, and Hirobumi Ito and Toshimichi Okubo hurried home to obtain one, acutely embarrassed at having their ignorance of basic international law exposed. From the beginning then, the negotiations were ill-starred, and they continued in the same vein for four months. Finally the Americans demanded an end to the talks, as no agreement had been reached, and the Japanese left for Europe choking on tears of humiliation.

GOLDEN DAYS IN WASHINGTON

> The five princesses are still at the residence of Mr. Charles
> Lanman, No. 120 West Street, Georgetown, where they will
> remain for some time in the charge of Mr. Lanman. They
> are attired in American costume and have already acquired
> many of the habits of the American people, having been
> under the charge of Minister DeLong in their own country.
> It is said they parted from the minister with great reluctance,
> as a very warm friendship had existed between them and Mrs.
> DeLong. One of the young ladies has a brother in this coun-
> try, attending school, who has been here some time.
> (*Evening Star*, March 4, 1872)

Sutematsu and her companions received the same attentive coverage in Washington as they had in San Francisco. Conscious that
they were representing Japanese womanhood they supplemented
their manners, already deemed charming, with a newly acquired
knowledge of Western social graces.

Once the delegation had left Washington the girls became the
responsibility of Mori, whose idea it had been, along with Kiyotaka Kuroda, to bring them to the United States in the first place.
However, Mori found himself in a dilemma—he was single and
had no idea how to look after five young girls. Umeko Tsuda was
only seven years old and particularly in need of a motherly figure.
For all his advocacy of women's education, Mori was woefully
unprepared for the practical consequences of his enlightened sug-
gestions.

It was Mori's secretary Charles Lanman who came to the res-
cue. With no children of their own, he and his wife offered to
look after the girls until more permanent homes were found for
them. Lanman not only worked at the Japanese legation but was in
fact an expert on the country of his employers. The Lanmans lived
in peaceful and picturesque Georgetown, Washington, D.C.,

where the red brick homes of high-ranking government officials were also located, secluded behind rows of poplar trees. The girls had been living out of suitcases since leaving Japan, and were pleased to be in a real home again, particularly since the Lanmans treated them like daughters. Taking care of five of them was quite a task even for the kindly couple, so Sutematsu, Shigeko, and Teiko moved to the home of Mrs. Lanman's sister, Mrs. Hepburn. Mr. Hepburn was the brother of James Hepburn, who invented the system of writing Japanese in Roman letters. Despite this separation, the girls continued to do everything together. No set schedules bound them, so every day they threw themselves into the task of learning American customs. They ceased to wear the kimonos they had brought from Japan, and instead dressed in clothes they had bought in America.

Before they realized, two months of this idyllic existence had passed. Deciding he could no longer take advantage of the Lanman's goodwill, Mori rented a house on Washington's Connecticut Avenue and moved the girls there, hiring a cook and an English teacher to live in with them. After two hours of English instruction in the morning, and apart from piano lessons once a week, the girls were free to do what they liked.

On Sundays they visited Mori, who after helping them with their English studies, showed them the sights of Washington in early summer. Driving down the poplar-lined avenues by carriage and eating packed lunches in one of the many grassy squares around the city, the girls were able to forget the gravity of their mission in America. Umeko was later to describe this period as "the golden days."

As summer turned into autumn, however, the health of the two older girls began to deteriorate. Quite simply, they were homesick. Homesickness of course does not strike when the traveler first encounters a foreign culture: there is too much that is new to see and do. It appears unexpectedly, after one has become used to a new way of life. Ryoko had been suffering from unexplained problems with her eyes since arriving in the States, and the fear of not being able to continue studying had compounded her homesickness. Teiko had been unwell since the end of summer, and had a slight but persistent fever.

In addition to their health problems, they could not forget that the empress had asked them to do their best as representatives of all their countrywomen, and that they were being supported by the taxpayers of Japan: how could they go home with their mission unfulfilled? Yet, Mori had no choice but to send them home, and at the end of October, Teiko and Ryoko returned to Japan, accompanied by the wife of an American chemist, an employee of the Hokkaido Development Bureau.

For years the remaining three girls lost track of their unfortunate companions. In the autumn of 1918 they finally found Teiko living in Ueno, Tokyo, married to a doctor. They went to visit her, and on meeting her friends of so many years before, Teiko broke down, telling them tearfully how "sad and ashamed" she had felt whenever she heard news of their successes. The other three women were at a loss to comfort her. Ryoko Yoshimasu opened a school for female English teachers in 1885, but died tragically the following year when a cholera epidemic swept Japan.

Mori had nursed doubts about the wisdom of keeping the five girls together from the moment he moved them into the house on Connecticut Avenue. From morning till night they were never apart, and anyone could see they were having a marvelous time, in addition to which Mrs. Lanman was always available to help. However, apart from their two hours of English lessons per day, the girls spoke almost exclusively in Japanese, and at this rate it would be a long time before they were competent enough English speakers to attend normal classes. Mori began the search for host families to take the girls. Sutematsu and Shigeko were placed in the family of the Reverend Leonard Bacon of New Haven, Connecticut, and Umeko returned to the Lanmans', where she had always been a favorite.

A New Daughter for
the Bacons

THE SEARCH FOR
A HOST FAMILY

When I first began researching Sutematsu's life story, I was greatly interested in how she came to live with the Bacon family. On reaching New Haven, I dived into the Yale archives, and as I read everything I could lay my hands on concerning the Reverend Leonard Bacon, the story began to unravel.

The latter half of the 1840s had seen the California gold rush, bringing with it a phenomenal increase in the wealth of the United States. The North's victory in the Civil War of the 1860s in turn paved the way for a capitalist free-enterprise system throughout the nation and encouraged big business. A hundred years after independence, the United States of the 1870s had entered that exclusive club of the world's most powerful nations for the first time. Though the average American citizen of the time knew little about Japan, American intellectuals were secure enough, intellectually

73

and psychologically, to look outside their own borders. Within their small group were a few who had a growing interest in the Far East.

A group involved in the study of China, Japan, and India had in fact existed in New York since the mid 1850s: the American Oriental Society. The Society counted among its members one Addison Van Name, who in 1865 began a forty-year career as a librarian at Yale. During that period he amassed a huge collection of works dealing with Far Eastern topics—in both quality and quantity the largest in America. Van Name spoke Mandarin and was well versed in Japanese history, so naturally he became acquainted with Sutematsu's brother Kenjiro during his time at Yale. When Mori asked Kenjiro to help him find host families for the girls, it is not difficult to imagine that Kenjiro would have spoken to Van Name before anyone else. (Several letters in which Kenjiro refers to this matter are stored in the university archives.)

At the same time Mori himself was canvassing his own acquaintances in New Haven: former Yale president Theodore Woolsey, who had given Mori valuable advice when he was pondering the best course for Japanese education, Connecticut Education Board chairman Birdsey Northrop, and the previously mentioned William Whitney, professor of linguistics at Yale. Whether they were fully aware of it at the time or not, both Mori and Kenjiro had entrusted the search for homes for Sutematsu and Shigeko to some of the most renowned intellectuals in America, who also happened to be among the few people with a detailed knowledge of the Orient.

By a strange coincidence, each one of them, including Van Name, had a connection with the Bacon family. Woolsey had been a classmate of Leonard Bacon at Yale, and his daughter Mary was married to Alfred, ninth child of the Bacons. Northrop's wife was a sister of Bacon's second wife, and Whitney lived directly opposite the family. Van Name was Bacon's brother-in-law, and met him often at gatherings of the Oriental Society.

The Reverend Leonard Bacon was born in Detroit in 1802.

When Sutematsu and Shigeko came to his home he was already seventy-one, and the father of fourteen children from two marriages. After graduating from Yale and Andover Theological Seminary, he settled in New Haven and took up the post of minister at Center Church, a Congregational church, where he remained for the next forty years. His sermons and speeches were of a high caliber, and he soon gained the respect of the townspeople as a man of learning. Bacon was also a well-known antislavery campaigner, never forgetting the horror of the slave auctions held outside his church in his youth. He spearheaded a movement to return black slaves to their African homeland and raised money for a black school in the town. By the time the Civil War began Bacon had already retired from his position as minister of Center Church, but he kept up a virulent campaign against the South, writing frequent letters to the religious paper *Independent*, of which he had once been an editor. Abraham Lincoln, upon entering the presidential race, made election speeches based on Bacon's book *The Evils of Slavery*. By the time Sutematsu came to live with the Bacons, he was lecturing in the theology department of Yale on the history of churches in America and on church policies.

The Reverend Leonard Bacon enjoyed a respected position in New Haven society, but the family's economic position was never as secure. The nine children of Bacon's first marriage had either died or left home, and only the oldest, Rebecca, aged about fifty, remained in the house. The five children by his second wife, Catherine, the youngest of whom was Alice, were all teenagers who needed to be fed and clothed.

During his years as a minister, Bacon had been on a salary of one thousand dollars per annum, roughly twenty dollars a week, so it is reasonable to assume that his salary at Yale was about the same amount. If the family took Shigeko and Sutematsu in there would be ten mouths to feed, making life even more difficult than it already was. Why then did Leonard Bacon answer Mori's plea?

The family's dire financial straits had something to do with

Bacon's response. Japanese government students were paying considerable sums, usually about fifteen dollars a week, to stay in American homes. If the Bacons agreed to have Sutematsu and Shigeko their income would more than double, and the family's existence would actually be more comfortable than before. That was certainly one reason Northrop and Van Name had in asking the Bacons to help. A letter written by Rebecca Bacon to her father, who was spending the summer in the countryside, throws more light on the situation.

July, 1872
Dear Father,

I went to see Mrs. Van Name about the little Jap. She was very glad to hear that we perhaps would like Miss Yamakawa and will write to her brother right away. In the meantime, some one may have snapped her up, but that is not likely. I told her that Mr. Van Name and B. G. Northrop might say what they thought would be a fair price for her and you would see. The young men around Washington pay for board and teaching $15.00 per week. . . .

Hatchigoochie [Hashiguchi], who has been Mrs. Porter's pupil and is at New Milford with her, is very sick indeed. They don't stand this climate too well and there is that responsibility to be counted in about this child. She will require watchful care. They are puny folks and can hardly lift the end of a trunk—the men. But they selected healthy ones to send over. . . .

[Kenjiro] Yamakawa does not want her to go to school—did not want her to come to this country at all—thought she was too young. She is the small heathen in the middle of the picture of five Japanese girls in *Harper's Weekly* on March 16. I think the girls can teach her and that Mother will find her an amusement when the girls are busy and away. . . .

Rebecca

Rebecca was directly involved in negotiations concerning the two girls. Over the summer, correspondence flowed back and forth between the Bacons, Van Name, and Kenjiro Yamakawa. By autumn Mori was discussing the practical details of the arrangement with Leonard Bacon. The following is a memo sent by the reverend to Mori:

Hon. Mr. Mori   New Haven
                                      Oct. 31, 1872

Dear Sir,

I respectfully submit to you the following memorandum of the conditions on which the two Japanese young ladies are this day received into my family, and of the care and responsibility which we as a family assume in their behalf.

1. We (Mrs. Bacon and myself) receive them not as mere boarders and lodgers, but as if they were the children of some near friend, who would expect us to have a parental care over them, and to treat them with all parental kindness—or as if they were our grandchildren. Mrs. Bacon and my daughters will be watchful over the health, morals, and manners of these young ladies, and will take care that their training is like that of daughters in the best New England families. We expect them to acquire that knowledge of domestic duties and employments which qualifies an American Lady to become the mistress of a family. . . . Till they have sufficiently acquired the use of the English language, and it shall be thought best for them to attend some school or to receive lessons at home under masters, they will be learning from my wife and daughters the art of reading and writing in English, and as much of Arithmetic and Geography as will prepare them to enter a suitable school. When they shall have learned to read English with sufficient facility, we shall take care to interest their minds in such books as will be useful to them.

2. My understanding is that for boarding, lodging, washing

and all their care and instruction, the compensation is to be fifteen dollars a week for each of the two young ladies, payable quarterly, namely for the first quarter at the end of six weeks or on the 12th of December, and thereafter on the 12th of March, June and September.

3. Medical advice and aid in case of illness, with other extra-ordinary expenses thus arising, will be an additional charge and will be met in the quarterly payment next succeeding.

4. Instruction on the piano will be given, at present, if desired, by competent teachers in my family and the charge for instruction, with the use of the instrument, will be at the rate of forty dollars for a year to each of them. Whenever Mr. Mori, or his successor in the guardianship of the young ladies, shall determine to employ a professional music teacher, the charge for the use of the piano will be to each of them eight dollars a year.

5. I reserve the power of annulling these arrangements at any time after giving six weeks' notice, and I concede the same power to Mr. Mori or his successor.

> I have the honor to be
> Very respectfully yours,
> Leonard Bacon

P.S. I have omitted to mention that the books and stationery, pencils, etc. for young ladies will be a separate charge in the account of their expenses; and that Mrs. Bacon will purchase for them, at their expense, all necessary articles of apparel so that they shall continue to be dressed in a style suitable to young ladies in a family like ours. If an allowance is made to each of $150 a year for clothing and incidental expenses, we will make the expenditure as much less than that amount as we can with due regard to propriety, and promise it will not be more than the allowance.

With its references to exact figures and payment details, the letter matters dealt with in a practical manner—considered the most trustworthy method of doing things. Leonard Bacon did in fact follow his memo to the letter. He looked after Sutematsu for the six years until she entered college, and treated her not as a guest, but as one of his own daughters. Given the same love and attention as the Bacon children received, the young girl from Japan grew up to be a credit to the family.

No mention of religion is made in the memo, but as the greater part of Leonard Bacon's life had been spent serving God and spreading the Christian message, Christianity would naturally play some part in Sutematsu's life in the Bacon household. Religion was in fact Kenjiro's greatest source of concern when he was deciding whether or not to let his sister be placed in the Bacon family. In a letter to Van Name he stressed that while Sutematsu was permitted to attend church services, she was to be given no religious instruction. Becoming a Christian would entail some form of penalty from the Japanese government, he added, so he wished that Sutematsu's religious education be left untampered with. As government students studying at public expense, it was important that he and his sister obey Japanese law.

Kenjiro himself was of the opinion that Christianity was inferior to Confucianism, and never attended a church service once during his entire stay in the United States. Rebecca Bacon made the following comments concerning Kenjiro's stubborn dislike of Christianity in a letter to her father:

> He would have no objections to her taking the order of things in a Christian family but would not like anything like direct attempts to proselyte. . . . He thinks the Bible is very well, but its precepts not so high as those of Confucius—as for instance when it says that a man may leave Father & Mother and cleave to his wife. He will be more liberal when he has been here longer.

In the end, Kenjiro need not have been concerned about his sister breaking Japanese law. Iwakura reported from Europe that unless the Japanese government took the laws banning Christianity off the statutes, Japan would never be treated equally by Western nations, and as things stood he had no hope of renegotiating any treaties. The Meiji government heeded Iwakura's advice and took steps to abolish the laws in February 1873. It is interesting to note that the new law was based on a first draft written by Leonard Bacon himself. The reverend wrote a letter to his son, also named Leonard, describing his work on that draft.

December 9, 1872

Dear Leonard,

. . . When Mr. Mori, the Japanese minister, was here about six weeks ago, he had been preparing a memorial to his government on the question of religious liberty, appending to the memorial of his draft a "Religious Charter" for the Empire. He submitted it, for consideration and advice, to a select number of gentlemen convened for the purpose by Secretary Northrop. Some of us felt his ideas on the subject were neither so clearly conceived nor so convincingly presented as was desirable in such a document; and at the suggestion of Mr. Northrop I took the matter in hand and devoted two or three days to it. I made an entirely new paper, memorial, charter and all.

I sent my paper, through Mr. Northrop, to Mr. Mori, with the message that he was at liberty to use it as he might please, and to incorporate just as much of it into his revised memorial as he might think desirable. I only requested that as I retained no copy he would return my manuscript when he should have done with it. The result was that he adopted my paper bodily, and sent it in for autograph to the Prime Minister, sending me a very fair copy made by one of his secretaries at the legation in Washington. If you hear in the course of a few months, that the Mikado has proclaimed a charter of religious liberty, you may not unreasonably presume that the Magna Charta of Japan was translated from my draft.

It is rather ironic that Kenjiro, who had a mortal fear of his sister being converted to Christianity, unknowingly placed her in the home of the man who as good as wrote the laws that finally forced the Japanese government to recognize religious freedom.

Sutematsu was baptized at Center Church in 1876 at age sixteen. Shigeko and Umeko also were baptized during their time abroad. Although each of the girls was brought up in strongly Christian environments, and although conversion may have seemed prearranged by their respective host families, no evidence of pressure exists. The girls were allowed to make their own decision.

The concepts of love for one's fellow human being and spiritual freedom that the girls learned through Christian teachings were reciprocal with Confucian beliefs that had long been a part of Japanese society. The three were to be greatly disappointed upon their return to Japan, however, when they observed a government that purportedly was in a hurry to build a Western-style "wealthy country and strong army" but outrightly ignored one of the basic tenets of Western political and social philosophy—Christian thought. Sutematsu, Shigeko, and Umeko, each in her individual way, were to work stubbornly over the years to change Japanese views of morality.

THE CITY OF ELM TREES

The center of New Haven has hardly changed in the past century, and even now visitors could easily find their way around using a map from a hundred years ago. The site of the Bacon home at 247 Church Street is now a parking garage, but by all accounts the original house, later used by the Reverend Leonard Bacon's grandchildren, stood until 1939, and stayed much the same as when Sutematsu was living there.

The town of New Haven was established in 1638 when a party of Puritans from Massachusetts settled in the area. Compared with the founders of many other New England towns, the early settlers had few problems with the local native Americans, and managed to purchase land peacefully. Blessed with abundant land for pasture, the town is located at the mouth of the Quinnipiac, Mill, and West rivers, facing the Long Island coast—an ideal position for a commercial port. With its natural advantages, New Haven was described as "the colony with the most capital and the most food."

The first settlers divided the nine acres they had purchased from the local people into nine sections, and proceeded to build magnificent two-story houses worthy of their prosperity. The middle section was left as a village green and used for markets and as a meeting area. Even today it acts as a resting place for the townspeople and as a venue for parades and concerts.

The New Haven Colony consisted of devout Puritans, and their determination not to bow to the tyranny of the Anglican church bound them together. The Bible was their guide for every aspect of life, from family matters to government: to them it contained God's instructions for the behavior of every individual, as well as every organization and system in society. Unlike the governments of the other colonies, this one was very theocratic in character, and only church members had the right to vote and the right to govern. Later, when New Haven merged with the Connecticut Colony, the settlers were forced to separate church and government, but for over a hundred years the town was administered from church buildings.

Puritan influence is still found in New Haven: three different churches stand around the green, but not one of them contains a crucifix or an icon, objects that were anathema to the Puritans. Even today, a Christmas tree cannot be erected on the green until after Thanksgiving, because the first settlers did not celebrate Christmas: giving thanks for a successful harvest was the far more important custom.

Charles Dickens visited New Haven in 1868, and was so impressed by Hillhouse Street that he declared it "the most beautiful street in America." James Hillhouse was the town's largest owner of land and businesses. In 1792 he took a shovel and began to plant elm trees all around his house; for several years after he continued planting them, with the help of local citizens, near the green, on the Yale campus, and around the houses on all the main streets, to protect the buildings from damage caused by sand blowing in from the sea. When he had finished, New Haven was known quite justifiably as the "City of Elms."

By the time the American Civil War broke out, New Haven had become Connecticut's largest city, with a population of forty thousand, and boasted fourteen banks and over five hundred shops. Four railway lines ran through the city, and travelers could go to New York and back with ease. Every home had gas lighting and running water, and the citizens of New Haven enjoyed one of the highest living standards in the country.

ARRIVAL AT THE BACON HOME

On October 30, 1872, Sutematsu and Shigeko said goodbye to Umeko and boarded the night train to New Haven with Mori. It was a year since they had left Japan, and today they would leave Mori, who had looked after them like a father for the past months, to live in a town they had never seen, with people they had never met. The girls were nervous, and spoke little, but Sutematsu was unable to hide her excitement: she was going to meet her brother Kenjiro, whom she had not laid eyes on since the Aizu War.

The journey took ten hours, and when they arrived in New Haven they found that a crowd of local people had gathered to welcome them. The following morning The *New Haven Morning Journal* described the scene:

Mr. Mori, minister from the Japanese Empire to this country, paid a visit yesterday under escort and by invitation of Secretary Northrop, to the Dwight School, the Skinner School, and the High School. The minister was highly pleased with what he saw and heard relative to our schools, and with our beautiful city. . . . The two Japanese boys were under the care of Mr. Northrop, of West Haven, with whom they reside. The two girls have just arrived in New Haven, and are domiciled at Rev. Dr. Bacon's where they are to reside.

The Reverend Leonard Bacon recorded in his diary on that day: "Two Japanese girls came today." Later he wrote to his son in Switzerland about them, in the same letter in which he had described his work on the draft for religious freedom.

. . . It was arranged at one time that two of the Japanese young ladies should be in our family, and they were both with us for the first week after their arrival in New Haven. But the consideration that they would not learn to speak English so rapidly if they were together prevailed, and one of them is now at Mr. Abbot's in Fair Haven. We were sorry to part with her eminently Mongolian features and her propensity to see the comical side of things. She was almost the more interesting one. But the other, Miss Stemats Yamakawa, charmed us all with her simplicity, her intelligence, and her affectionately confiding ways. Even the Celtic inmates of the house are evidently fond of her, and if they are aware that she is a "haythen," that makes no difference to them. Thus far I do not believe that anybody in the family has had occasion to find fault with her. Your mother gives her lessons every day, devoting several hours of the morning to her. Nelly is her music teacher, and will receive her own compensation at the rate of $40 per annum. We receive for board, lodging, care and teaching $15 a week.

A week after their arrival Shigeko and Sutematsu were split up to facilitate their English study, and for the first time since they landed in America the girls were apart and forced to acclimate by themselves.

Sutematsu was soon off to a good start as a member of the Bacon household. She became friends with the youngest daughter, Alice, who was two years her senior, and before long they were like real sisters. Mrs. Bacon's weak constitution confined her to the house for much of the time, so she took special pleasure in teaching the quiet Japanese girl, who was attentive and a fast learner. Sutematsu seemed to give the reverend's wife a new lease on life, and for the rest of the family too, she was like a breath of fresh air.

SUTEMATSU THE TOMBOY

Supported by the affectionate care of her host family, Sutematsu adjusted smoothly to life in New Haven. She had numerous playmates her own age in the neighborhood, and became particularly friendly with Marian Whitney, daughter of Yale professor William Whitney. Whether studying or playing, the two girls were together almost every day. In later years Marian went on to obtain a master's degree at Yale and teach German at Vassar College. Remaining single all her life, she devoted herself to the cause of women's education. She described the time she spent with Sutematsu in New Haven in the Vassar alumni magazine, the *Vassar Quarterly*, over forty years later:

July 1919
The Bacon home was just across the street from my own and the coming of the little foreigner, only a couple of years my senior, was a great excitement to me and my companions. She was soon received into our midst on equal terms and was for several years my schoolmate and playmate. She was a slender, graceful little creature, full of life and spirit and willing to take part in every game; a swift runner, a good climber, and later a marvellous swimmer. I remember how, when we

began to learn to dive, her lithe figure would spring into the air from the little raft and go down straight as an arrow into the water, while we splashed and floundered and fell flat upon the surface.

Intellectually Stematz soon equalled the girls of her age, in spite of the handicap of language and early background. She was fitted for college in the New Haven High School, taking the full classical course. In addition to this her brother, then a student in the Sheffield Scientific School at Yale, finding that his little sister was forgetting her mother tongue, wisely insisted on giving her weekly lessons in Japanese and I remember her complaint that they were harder than anything else she had to do.

Sutematsu running around with her skirts hitched up, Sutematsu climbing trees like a monkey: it was a very different image from the one of later years—photographs with titles such as *Sutematsu— wife of Marquis Oyama* and *The Flower of the Rokumeikan*—showing her with a stern, almost unfriendly expression. In New Haven, Sutematsu was free to indulge in tomboy games, but Japanese society did not allow women to act in such a way. It may be that when she returned to Japan some of Sutematsu's desires were buried forever, relegated to the past.

Though they lived in different towns, Sutematsu, Shigeko, and Umeko were able to see each other from time to time. Two years after the shift to New Haven, during the Christmas holidays of 1874, Connecticut Board of Education chairman Northrop took Sutematsu and Shigeko to Washington, where they spent a few days with Umeko at the Lanman home. A heartwarming letter written in a beautiful hand, which Sutematsu sent to her host mother Mrs. Bacon, remains: the English is surprisingly good for someone who had spent only two years with an American family.

Georgetown, D.C.
Dec. 20th, 1874

My very dear Mrs. Bacon,

It is really rainy day so that we did not go to the church and I did not have any thing to read. I thought I write to you a short letter.

Our journey was pretty comfortable, though Shige and I had to sleep together.

About one o'clock in the morning Shige thought it was the time to wake up and dress, so she got up and dressed, but we did not come to Washington so she slept again.

At seven o'clock we arrived at Georgetown, and all my friends were very glad to see us.

Yesterday morning we went to see Mrs. Yano. She is boarding now for the new minister has come, with his wife.

The new minister's wife went to the president's reception with Japanese [*unintelligible*]. I have not seen her yet for the legation is in such confusion that we will be in their ways.

Washington has been improved very much since I saw it last.

Saturday morning we thought we will go to the President's house and see the inside, but Mrs. Lanman thought it was too early in the morning to go in, so we did not.

Last night Mrs. Lanman's friends came to see us, and I had to play new plays for them and then what they wanted me to play on the piano.

I was afraid that I would make so many mistakes, and I could not play anything decent, but I tried and I did not make many mistakes. Shige played hers very nicely. Ume is as talkative as ever. She can read and recite poetry very well and it was true that she received four prizes. Do you not remember that we read about it in newspaper in October?

Day before yesterday we ate an orange as big as your breakfast plates, and inside of it was as red as my new dress. It was very good, and we ate it with sugar.

After dinner I can not write to you any more for I ate so much oysters that I can not write.

Give my love to all and I send two kisses for last night and tonight.

When are you going to New York?

From your loving daughter
Stematz Yamakawa

P.S. I made good many mistakes in spelling and grammar for Mrs. Lanman was down stairs and I could not ask her.

This letter illustrates the depth of the relationship which had already formed between the girl and her host mother.

Mrs. Lanman also wrote to Sutematsu's host mother, after the girls had returned home.

Georgetown D.C.
Feb. 6th, 1875

My Dear Mrs. Bacon,

In reply to your kind letter thanking us for our kindness to Stematz, I feel that I cannot say enough to give you the extent of our interest in her as well as the other Japanese children whom we love so much.

You will, however, be pleased to know that your child of the three gave entire satisfaction to all among our acquaintances who met her, and who naturally commented favorably upon her personal appearance, manner and education so far as they were capable of judging.

Her music gave us great pleasure and she was commended for her politeness and good nature whenever called upon to play.

The truth is, we fell in love with her, and so far from being any trouble to us during their visit, both of the girls were very thoughtful and considerate, and did everything that they could to save trouble. We only hope they may be allowed to repeat this visit at some future time and gladden our home once more.

I agree with you in thinking it a strange dispensation of Providence that these children should be sent to us, and especially to myself who have had no experience in the training of children, and I tremble sometimes at the responsibility which I took with the charge of Ume.

I can only hope and pray that I may be enabled to perform the duty which daily presses upon me to lead her in the right path.

She is a most obedient and loving child and we are devotedly attached to her, our great sorrow will be to part with her when the time comes.

With kind regards to your family,

I am yours truly
Adeline Lanman

Nowadays, when students apply for study abroad, their language and general academic ability are first tested. That serves to narrow the field of candidates, and those who are successful at the first screening are interviewed and given health checks before the final decisions are made. Of course the Hokkaido Development Bureau had conducted no such tests—they could hardly afford to be choosy when two recruitment drives had attracted a mere five applicants. Although the two older girls were forced to return to Japan because of illness, the remaining three were marvelous advertisements for the new Japan, and a stroke of luck for the bureau. Or perhaps it was that the girls' parents had chosen a particular path for their daughters in the knowledge that they were equipped to manage life overseas.

Sutematsu herself was extremely fortunate: living in a town that gave such high priority to education, with a family of pious, caring people who shared everything with her. The experience helped to shape her into the intelligent, sophisticated woman that she was to become.

"OUR SOCIETY"

Sutematsu was admitted to Hillhouse, the local co-ed high school, in September 1875. She was fifteen years old. New Haven already had a long tradition of placing great importance on women's education, and intelligent girls were encouraged to attend high school, rather than follow the more prevalent pattern of marriage and housekeeping. The Bacons' daughter Alice was one who followed the first path. Due to economic restraints, she was unable to go on to college after graduating from Hillhouse High, but she persevered with her own study and managed to obtain the equivalent of a bachelor's degree from Harvard a year before Sutematsu graduated from Vassar College.

Sutematsu's high school days were happy and carefree, enough to make any present-day Japanese student wish he or she could go back in time and swap places. Just how carefree is illustrated by this extract from the diary of Sutematsu's friend Marian Whitney.

Feb. 1, 1876   Went to school in the morning. In the afternoon went down to Maria Trowbridges and then went down to Japanese store with Maria and Stematz. Studied all the evening.

Feb. 3   Had such a cold in head and throat that I stayed in bed all day until dinner when I dressed and went downstairs. Stematz came over and played checkers. My eyes were so weak that I could not read or write.

Feb. 8   Went to school. In the afternoon it snowed a little. I went over to Maria Trowbridges and skated in the yard with her, also Alice and Stematz. We sang and had a jolly time. Then we came over home and played Jumping Jack Jones.

Feb. 19   Went to school and studied French and Latin. In

the afternoon, went to sleighing with Stematz. In the evening knitted a sock.

In Sutematsu's time, over the years a privileged "class" of New Haven people had formed the "Hillhouse Society," to the exclusion of those less educated and wealthy in the town. Named after New Haven's favorite son, James Hillhouse, its members were the Yale president, professors, ministers, and businessmen, most of whom lived in palatial houses on Hillhouse Street. This elite group met every week at one of the member's homes, to discuss such matters as academic learning, art, and the progress of the town. They preferred their children's marriage partners to come from within the same circle, and predictably this little society did not allow just anyone to join. Nothing short of a miracle would have enabled the Reverend Leonard Bacon to live on Hillhouse Street, but the impecunious minister was accepted into the group as a respected intellectual and because his church, Center Church, had the highest status of any in the town.

The women of the "Hillhouse Society" had their own circle, known as "Our Society." "Extending a helping hand to destitute women and children" was the purpose of the society, which had been founded by a Mrs. Skinner, the wife of the mayor at the time, in 1833. Membership was restricted to the families of the "Hillhouse Society" and to those nominated by them. Six meetings were held a year, at which the women would discuss the information they had gathered since their last meeting and decide what work needed to be done. In Sutematsu's time they collected clothing for the families of immigrants who had fled the Franco-Prussian War, gave essential items to black women suffering from tuberculosis, and raised money for families whose male breadwinner was too sick to work, among other projects. At the time New Haven had no publicly funded welfare organizations, so the work of the women of "Our Society" was valuable, and respected accordingly.

Sutematsu participated in the group's activities as Alice's guest. She never missed a meeting, being happy to stitch diapers and make children's clothes. It was at those meetings that Sutematsu learned the meaning of volunteer work firsthand, and that women could use their abilities to make some contribution to society, that in fact it was their duty to do so.

In later years Sutematsu made use of that experience to organize Japan's first charity bazaar, a year after her marriage to Minister of War Iwao Oyama. The proceeds were to go toward the building of a nursing school for the present Jikei University School of Medicine Hospital in Tokyo. Sutematsu did an admirable job of organizing her group of upper-class Japanese women, who had never even heard of a bazaar until she explained what it was. The results far exceeded all expectations, and the event, held in the Rokumeikan, raised a considerable sum for the school. Novelty was certainly a factor in the bazaar's success: not only was it Japan's first example of volunteer activity, but it was run by women, most of whom had never handled money in their lives.

The year Sutematsu started high school, her brother Kenjiro returned to Japan. Kenjiro had been against his sister coming to the United States from the start, and when she did his greatest fear was that she would lose her love for Japan and become totally Americanized. Accordingly, after she moved to New Haven he made it a point to give her lessons in Japanese and in the teachings of Confucius every week. After returning home he wrote to his sister frequently, the contents of his letters generally concerned with movements in the Japanese government and international politics. Sutematsu admitted to friends that she wished Kenjiro would tell her something about the family for a change.

In 1876, the year after his return, Kenjiro took up the post of assistant professor in the science department at Tokyo Kaisei School (now the University of Tokyo). The same year he wrote the following letter to the Bacons:

Tokio, Japan.
Apr. 21st, 1876

Dr. & Mrs. Bacon,
My dear Sir & Madam,

Since I wrote last year I have been neglecting the obligation of friendship in letter writing, which you must be lenient in excusing as you know very well the nature of our nation, who are not much reputed for being unlazy (if you excuse me to use such a term). You will wrong me however, if you were to think [*unintelligible*] to forget a friend, which is, you must own, not National characteristics of Japanese people.

You might hear, how I am [*unintelligible*] away my time from Stematz to whom I have written a long letter.

What I want to tell you is about the silk, which you, Mrs. Bacon, wished [me] to send. To tell you the truth, I wanted to make a present of it to you, for which reason I did not take the money which you wanted to entrust to me. Since my return to this country, I have been reduced to a great poverty and have not been able to execute my design. I think you will not think me very unkind, and now ask you whether you want the silk of your description or of some other quality. & I hope you will be kind enough to tell me that by next mail.

You will not, I hope, refuse to accept it, and if you are to accept it at all, you will let me know what sort of silk is best or whether that quality which you spoke of when I left New Haven still suits you or no, and what will be more convenient & thus I can increase my poor acknowledgement for the great kindness and diligent care that you have taken over my sister.

My mother particularly send her respect to you & wish to express her gratitude to you.

I am yours truly,

Kenjiro Yamakawa
Kai-sei-gak-ko
Tokio, Japan

P.S. Please give my kind regards to your sons & daughters.

After the feudal domains were replaced by the modern prefectural system in 1871, the Yamakawa family left Tonami and went to
live in rental accommodations in downtown Tokyo. Hiroshi joined
the army and became a major three years later, but prejudice
against the Aizu still remained, making it almost impossible for him
to obtain a good promotion. Adding to his problems were the students who arrived in the capital from Tonami and relied on the
Yamakawas for room and board. One of those students was Goro
Shiba, who later rose to the rank of general, despite his Aizu background. At the age of fourteen he had left the hand-to-mouth
existence in Tonami for Tokyo, and in 1875 passed the examination allowing him to enter the military preparatory academy there.
Until the school year began he had nowhere to live, and ended up
staying with the Yamakawas. Here he tells what life was like for the
family:

> The only task they gave me was messenger, so I had a lot of
> free time. I was treated like one of the family, however the
> Yamakawas were very poor in those days, and I was usually
> sent to the pawn shop in Asakusa several times a month with
> articles to pawn. Food supplies were meager, and tofu and
> cooked beans were both great luxuries.
>
> One day I was summoned by the head of the household
> and his mother, Mrs. Yamakawa, who said, 'We're terribly
> sorry, but you can see what dire straits the family is in. I won-
> der if you could lend us some of the money you have saved.'
>
> A former chief retainer was borrowing money from some-
> one like me, the equivalent of a servant! . . . I couldn't believe

it. I had no objections, of course, so I agreed, and they thanked me profusely. I didn't know what to say. The money was the nest egg I had brought from Aomori with me, a total of thirteen yen and fifty sen [about thirteen dollars today]. (Mahito Ishimitsu, *Aru Meijijin no kiroku*.)

With the family as destitute as that, it is little wonder that Kenjiro was unable to buy the promised silk for Mrs. Bacon. However, after he entered the University of Tokyo as an assistant professor, he worked his way up to become president in 1901. Kenjiro could hardly have done more to fulfill the promise he made as a student to his Yale classmate's aunt who lent him money: he had indeed worked hard for his country.

Leaving the Nest

VASSAR COLLEGE

$\mathcal{S}$utematsu was nineteen and ready to sit for her college entrance exams. Women's colleges of the day set very tough tests for prospective students, and demanded the same level of academic ability as the men's colleges. In her final year at Hillhouse High Sutematsu chose the college preparatory course, throwing herself into intense study. On the suggestion of Mr. Northrop of the Connecticut Board of Education, she spent her summer vacation visiting various colleges, such as Smith and Wellesley in Massachusetts, but finally settled on Vassar, the school which, six years earlier, Japanese Minister Arinori Mori had recommended as the best women's college in the United States in terms of academic achievement.

Located in the small town of Poughkeepsie, about sixty miles up the Hudson River from New York, Vassar College was founded by businessman Matthew Vassar, who had amassed a huge fortune in brewing.

Vassar believed that women are blessed with the same intelligence as men, and therefore have the same right to a higher education, and he demonstrated his beliefs by building a college exclusively for women. Strange that a beer baron should be associated with one of the most prestigious women's colleges on the East Coast, but his unusual choice of women's education as a cause ensured that his name would live on in academic circles all over the world; if he had simply bequeathed his money to the town, the businessman would have been remembered only by the residents of Poughkeepsie. It is said that at the first meeting of the newly appointed Board of Trustees, Vassar threw a tin box containing $408,000 worth of deeds and securities on the table and declared, "This is one-half of everything I own, use it as you please: from today I leave the running of the college entirely up to you."

In 1861 the state of New York granted permission to begin construction of the college, and on June 4 the first stone was laid. The onset of the Civil War halted progress on the site, so that it was not until four years later, in the summer of 1865, that the buildings were completed.

The main building was modelled on the luxurious Tuileries of Paris. The college boasted excellent facilities, including an observatory, gymnasium, and riding school. It was also the first university in the world to have central heating. On September 26, 1865, Vassar College opened its doors to fifty students from all over America, beginning an illustrious history in women's education.

Thirteen years later, in 1878, the college's first Asian student to study for a bachelor's degree joined the ranks of the thirty-eight entrants. The college directory of 1878 recorded the occasion as follows:

1878 September 18
Shige Nagai, special student and Stematz Yamakawa, '82 came as students to Vassar at the expense of the Japanese government. As little girls, they had come to the U.S. in 1871 with

the first Embassy of Japan to the Great Powers. [Miss Yamakawa was the first Asian woman to take an American college degree.]
("The Magnificent Enterprise—A Chronicle of Vassar College," 1961)

After six years with the Bacons, a new phase in Sutematsu's life was about to begin. She later described her time at Vassar as "the happiest four years of my life, and the most full of hope."

The girls from "the land of the Mikado" were popular students. At first that may have been due to their exotic value, but as college life settled down into its usual routine, Sutematsu and Shigeko, who were quite different from each other in personality and looks, began to win the admiration of their classmates for their individual qualities, not simply because they were Asian and Japanese.

A friend of the Abbot family, with whom Shigeko had been placed, later wrote the following article about the two girls and their life at Vassar, entitled "Japanese Vassar Girls":

> In the autumn of 1879, when they had been there a year, I went to Vassar. A daughter-in-law of Dr. Abbot's was one of my dearest friends. It secured me their immediate acquaintance. Stematz was exclusive. She was very brilliant. Shige was very sweet. They both wore European dress. Sutematz looked like a beautiful Jewess of a poetic type. Shige was broadly and indubitably Japanese. Sutematz was president of her class in her sophomore year. She wrote charming essays. Shige was never president of anything. But every one loved her. She was invaluable at our fortnightly "candy pulls." She was splendid on sleigh ride. She spent half her leisure coddling the sick girls in the infirmary. I have no memory of an hour's indisposition at Vassar that I did not hear the click, click of Shige's funny little walk as she came down the corridor bringing me a pitcher of lemonade and unlimited sympathy. I never saw

Sutematz excited, though two red spots always flamed on her cheeks and her hand shook as she thrust it through the window of our college postoffice. I have never seen Shige when she wasn't excited. Sutematz was very beautiful from every standpoint. She was slim, and tall for a Japanese woman. . . . Sutematz played a wonderful game of chess and excelled every professor in the faculty at whist. . . . Once a day they secluded themselves in their "parlor" and spoke Japanese for an hour. Sutematz was fanatic in her observance of this and compelled Shige to be as regular. Sutematz wrote a letter "home" every day. Shige had all a school girl's horror of letter writing.
(*Sunday Advertiser*, October 1, 1893)

Unlike Japan, where students study extremely hard to enter their desired university but once admitted attend classes only when they feel like it, preferring to concentrate their energies on club activities and part-time work, American college students put a great deal of effort into their studies, and this is facilitated in part by the fact that most live on campus. When the workload becomes too heavy, or they have a problem of a more personal nature, American students often turn to their roommate. Long after the lights are supposed to be out they talk about life and love, or invite other friends in. The superintendent generally turns a blind eye, as long as others are not being disturbed. Living in dormitories is a large part of the college experience and is often what graduates remember most fondly about their school days.

Life at Vassar, a collection of photographs published in 1940 by the Vassar Cooperative Bookshop, includes pictures of the dormitory that were taken in Sutematsu's time. Inside each of the cosy rooms there is a walnut bed, a comfortable-looking sofa, and a mahogany desk. Decorated by their occupants in an unmistakably feminine fashion, the walls of each room are covered with photographs and paintings. The text explains that the residents were required to turn out their gas lamps by ten o'clock, but that "this rule was frequently broken."

Sutematsu loved her four years in the dormitory. After her return to Japan and marriage to Iwao Oyama, she often wrote to her fellow Vassar graduates and told them how much she wished she could once again see the dormitory that had provided her with so many happy memories: it was not to be, however, as she died without making a second visit to America. After her death, Sutematsu's classmates came up with the idea of establishing a memorial room—a reproduction of their Japanese classmate's room at Vassar—in her honor. Although almost fifty years had passed since their graduation, Sutematsu's classmates donated money for the purchase of furniture and fittings, and five years after the inception of the idea the "Princess Oyama Memorial Room" was opened in the Alumnae House. The memorial room contained photographs and articles used by Sutematsu, and the kimono that she wore to visit the imperial palace, sent by Shigeko, who had received it after Sutematsu's death.

Unfortunately, the room was knocked down when the Alumnae House was rebuilt in 1960. Apart from her kimono, Sutematsu's possessions and the other articles related to her time at Vassar are currently stored in the Special Collection Room at the college. Her kimono was donated to the Japan Society in New York, which in turn lent it to the Metropolitan Museum of Art for an exhibition of Japanese kimonos. Its whereabouts since then remains a mystery.

During her stay at Vassar, Sutematsu studied French, German, Latin, English composition, history, philosophy, chemistry, botany, and mathematics, and later specialized in physics, physiology, and zoology. Her grades were always among the highest, and in her second year she was elected class president. One of her duties in that capacity was to speak at the welcoming party held every year for new students, and she never failed to impress the newcomers with her witty speech. Turning up in a beautiful brightly colored kimono, she also dazzled the crowd in her role as marshal of the annual festivities held to commemorate Founder's Day. Sutematsu also found time to write several articles for the college magazine *Miscellany*, including one in her third year that outlined the political circumstances surrounding the Meiji Restoration in Japan. Though she was most likely influenced by her brother Kenjiro, the article reflects Sutematsu's surprisingly strong interest in her mother country, despite her ten-year absence.

Sutematsu was a favorite of her professors as well as of her fellow students, as illustrated by the following memoir of Professor of English Literature Helen Hiscock Backus:

> Few of the many who enjoyed the supple grace, the suavity, the seeming insouciance of the slender, brown, college student, would have predicted for her a great career. She was a modest, generous, funloving girl among girls, never claiming any patrician immunities, as she certainly never betrayed the loneliness of the alien. A sense of reserve power those felt who especially interested themselves in her development. When the class-room was depressed by that "sleepiness" which experienced teachers dread, Sutematz could confound her languid American classmates with a brilliant recitation in literature or logic. The English language of which she was mistress for all practical purposes, would be twisted somewhat awry by her surge of feeling, if some friends asked her to describe the scenes of her childhood, the spirit of Japanese home life, or indeed that system of selfish diplomacy by which the British so long depressed Japanese commerce and jurisprudence.
> (*Vassar Miscellany*, February 1901)

In the spring of 1881, the Japanese government ordered Sutematsu, Shigeko, and Umeko to come home. Their ten years were up. Shigeko returned to Japan on schedule: she had received a

"Testimonial" (certificate) after studying music for three years at Vassar. In addition, her health was not as good as it should have been, so all in all she had no objections to leaving.

Sutematsu, on the other hand, had only a year to go before she would be able to graduate with her classmates. Umeko also had a year's study remaining before she could receive a high school diploma from the Arthur Institute in Washington. The two girls requested that they be allowed to graduate, and received permission from the Japanese government to extend their stay another year.

THE VALEDICTORIAN

With only a limited time left, Sutematsu, although already at the top of her class, studied even harder, trying not to let her apprehension about going home interfere with her work. Shigeko, in her letters from Japan, described in her characteristically humorous way the things that had confused, frightened, and impressed her there, and Sutematsu was unable to hide her fear of returning to what was virtually an unknown land. During her time at Vassar, Shigeko had become acquainted with Sotokichi Uryu, a cadet at the U.S. Naval Academy, and after her return home the pair were engaged. Shigeko's letters were therefore overflowing with the excitement of a young woman on the eve of her marriage, and poor Sutematsu, who was older, no doubt began to feel uneasy. Her classmates noticed a subtle change in her mood, some writing later that they saw at that time a Sutematsu quite different from the confident woman they thought they knew.

Back in New Haven for her last Christmas vacation in the United States, Sutematsu experienced the unexpected loss of her eighty-year-old American father Leonard Bacon on Christmas Eve. The man had fulfilled his promise to Arinori Mori to the letter, and had brought Sutematsu up with the same measure of love and attention as his own daughters. Tragically, the Reverend Leonard Bacon had passed away without seeing his Japanese

daughter's graduation, but as may be seen from the letter that
Sutematsu wrote to Mrs. Bacon, he would always live on in her
heart.

> Thank you very, very much for the picture which you sent
> me. It is such a perfect likeness that every time I look at it I
> feel as if Dr. Bacon was speaking to me. It stands on my desk
> just above my head as I sit to read or write and as I look up, I
> am reminded of that noble and beautiful life, which had done
> so much for me. I am sure it will be a great help to me to
> have the picture for when I look at it I can not but wish to be
> good and true as he would wish to have me to be. . . .
>
> (Vassar College, January 28, 1882)

The June sun shone on the well-kept lawn of Vassar campus,
which was dotted with tiny saplings connected by silver and rose-
colored ribbons. The thirty-nine members of the class of 1882 had
planted the trees to commemorate their graduation on that day.

Today was the most important day in the Vassar calendar, and
the most exciting for its students: those still in college as well as
those about to say goodbye. The graduating students, decked out
in their best finery, were going from one professor to another,
thanking them for their teaching and guidance over the previous
four years. The young women's parents, who had traveled from all
over the United States to be present for their daughters' proud day,
watched with satisfied smiles. Decorations from the graduation ball
of the night before—which had continued until the small hours—
had been removed, and the interiors of the hall and chapel seemed
to shine brighter than usual.

At ten-thirty on the dot, the organ in the chapel struck up a
marching tune, signalling the entrance of the thirty-nine graduating students, followed by the president, the professors, and an
assortment of guests in a solemn procession ending on the stage.
Sutematsu, in her kimono, was seated ninth from the front. She

had been chosen as one of ten valedictorians and had prepared her speech on the topic "British Policy toward Japan." In the audience was Mr. Takahashi, the Japanese consul, who had come from New York for the graduation ceremony, which opened with a prayer from President Caldwell. One by one the valedictorians rose nervously and took the podium for their speeches: "The Conscience of Science," "The Perfidiousness of Alexander II," "The Decline of Speculative Philosophy," and so on. Each valedictorian tackled a difficult subject, as had come to be expected of Vassar graduates. The women were obviously confident and proud of the education they had received, which was second to none. They did not foresee that the roll of Vassar graduates would one day include the names of many pioneering women—the first ones to encroach on traditionally male domains: the first female graduate of M.I.T., the first female instructor at Stanford University, America's first female gynecologist, and, of course, the first Japanese woman to graduate from college.

When Sutematsu rose to give her speech, there was a sharp intake of breath as her elaborately embroidered kimono came into view. What Sutematsu had to say, however, impressed the audience even more. Her speech was interrupted frequently by applause. When she had finished, her listeners continued to clap for some time.

The *Poughkeepsie Eagle* carried a report of Sutematsu's speech the following morning.

> The next address was the most interesting of the whole series, being by Miss Sutematz Yamakawa, of Tokio, Japan, on "British Foreign Policy toward Japan." . . . Her address was an eloquent plea for the independent nationality of Japan. The selfish policy of England in all her dealings with the peoples of the East was described and denounced in severe terms. Behind the ostensible wish for the spread of Christianity and civilization is a desire to subject everything to the interest of

British trade, and if this cannot be accomplished otherwise, to reduce Japan to British control, and make it the younger sister of India, Cyprus and the Transvaal. She explained the effect of the rule of extraterritorial jurisdiction, as established by the treaties, under which a British subject in any of the ports opened to trade is entirely independent of Japanese law, and only under the jurisdiction of a British Secretary of legation. The [Japanese] government wishes to throw the whole country open to the commerce of the world, but if it does so it opens all to British law, and becomes powerless to protect itself and its people. The effect of the present policy was described as ruinous to Japan, and the speaker said that if it were carried farther, and the attempt were made to extend British power, there were countrymen of hers who would resist to the last drop of their blood, and would never cease to struggle for an independent national existence.

(June 15, 1882)

Since its founding, the United States had pursued a policy of isolationism, based on the Monroe Doctrine. Successive American governments had made it known that they would not interfere in the disputes and internal squabbles of the European nations, and warned that in return those nations should not make America an object of their imperialist ambitions. Thus Sutematsu's speech, calling for an end to England's invasive policy toward Japan, though not about U.S. policy, appealed to the audience's ideology and engendered a great deal of sympathy for Japan. The *New York Times* noted:

It was commented upon by the press at the time as showing remarkable prophetic intelligence. She thoroughly understood England's conservatism, and paid tribute to America's liberality and friendship.

(June 1882)

And the *Chicago Tribune* praised her speech as follows:

> "British Policy toward Japan" was the subject which Sutematz
> Yamakawa treated with such vigor and clearness, combined
> with such a forcible use of the purest Anglo-Saxon, as to
> make this the most notable, as it was the most enthusiastically
> applauded oration of the day.
> (June 22, 1882)

A month later the event was reported in the *Asahi Shinbun*
newspaper in Sutematsu's home country:

> The applause continued for some time, shaking the auditori-
> um, and forcing Miss Yamakawa to discontinue her speech.
> She tried to continue but choked with emotion momentarily
> forgot what she had been going to say. Never before had a
> foreigner's speech moved an American audience so much.
> Miss Yamakawa brought great honor not only to herself, but
> to her country.
> (July 29, 1882)

In her choice of international relations as the topic of her thesis,
Sutematsu had probably been influenced by her brother's constant
letters keeping her up-to-date on Japan's position in the world.
Her speech dealt head-on with Japan's problems in its relations
with other nations, and was daring in its total condemnation of
British foreign policy. It would have been interesting to hear the
opinions of Tomomi Iwakura and the other Japanese statesmen
who had spent two fruitless years trying to negotiate an end to the
unequal treaties. Surely they would have been impressed by
Sutematsu's speech.

THE CONNECTICUT TRAINING SCHOOL
FOR NURSES

The day after the ceremony, the thirty-nine new graduates said
goodbye to each other, and promising to meet again in the near

future, left to begin their new lives. Sutematsu's feelings were most likely more mixed than those of her classmates: soon she would be crossing the vast American continent and sailing back across the Pacific, without knowing whether she would ever again see the campus where she had been so happy. How many of those women with whom she had shared her joys and sorrows for four years would make it all the way to Japan to see her? What kind of life awaited her in the country she had left ten years before? Sutematsu left Vassar lonely and uncertain about what lay before her.

After spending some time in the Bacon household, Sutematsu entered the Connecticut Training School for Nurses at New Haven Hospital to attend classes. The Connecticut Training School for Nurses, one of the oldest of such institutions in the country, was established in 1873 by Yale medical school professor Francis Bacon, who was the second son of the Reverend Leonard Bacon, and his wife Georgeanna Bacon. It was probably through this connection that Sutematsu was allowed to attend the school for only the two months of July and August.

Georgeanna was a woman of diverse interests, and from her youth had been involved in politics and social issues, including the antislavery movement. During the Civil War she had tirelessly nursed in the hospitals of New York and Washington, as well as in the field hospitals of Gettysburg and other battlegrounds. The book she wrote, *A Handbook of Nursing for Family and General Use* (Philadelphia: Lippincott, 1879), was the definitive work on nursing, used by American hospitals and training schools for many years.

It was not an easy couple of months for Sutematsu. Apart from learning basic hygiene and techniques essential for a good grounding in nursing, the students spent time every day at the hospital, where they cooked up huge batches of beef and chicken broths on the order of the doctors, scrubbed the floors, and cleaned huge pots and even the coal shovels. The manual labor was mindless and boring, Sutematsu grumbled to Alice in a letter, but she enjoyed the actual nursing and thought she was suited to the work. It is not clear why she suddenly decided to obtain nursing skills, but it was likely on a suggestion of the Bacons, that she not waste the final two months of her stay. Judging from her good grades in physiology and biology, Sutematsu had some interest in the field, but she appeared to have no intention of taking up nursing as a career when she returned to Japan.

A letter that Sutematsu wrote to Alice in between preparing batches of soup at the New Haven Hospital kitchens reveals for the first time her thoughts of opening a girls' school with her host sister.

> I hope very earnestly that you will be able to come out to Japan next spring. I don't know whether your relatives will approve of your taking such a step, but I hope your wish to work with me for the good of Japan may be realized. You can do much here I know, but your opportunity to sacrifice yourself for the sake of others is indeed endless in Japan. Perhaps a few years will not be very long to your friends but in Japan you can do so much even in a year or two. It would be delightful if we could keep house together so that whenever any of the Bacon family should turn up, for I firmly believe that some of the members will eventually cross the Pacific[,] or when some of my school friends should be travelling in the East, we could ask them to stay with us and we could show them all around. Suppose now for instance you were to teach English language and literature and I—well what can I teach?—perhaps physiology and gymnastics. These being my present hobby, in the female Normal school, that is supposing we can't have a school of our own and then we could live together with perhaps my Mother to chaperone us if you don't object. . . . When the summer vacations come we might go north and visit the home of my childhood and further up to Yesso and see the Ainus since you are so much

interested in ethnology. But perhaps I am counting the chickens before they are hatched and building castles in the air. Still it is pleasant to think about it when there is no harm done by it.

(New Haven, August 2, 1882)

Whatever Sutematsu's motivation was for venturing into training to become a nurse, the knowledge she gained over those two months was to stand her in good stead on her return to Japan. At the time nursing in Japan was carried out exclusively by males and was considered a thoroughly disreputable and dirty occupation. It was Sutematsu who recognized the need for a school to train nurses, and who initiated Japan's first charity bazaar to raise funds for it. Moreover, when a volunteer nursing association was established by upper-class women as part of the Japanese Red Cross, it was Sutematsu who became the director and worked to promote the spread of hygiene and nursing methods, and raised the status of nurses.

HOMEWARD BOUND

In October 1882, after almost eleven years in America, Sutematsu and Umeko departed from New York on the start of their long trek home. Sutematsu was twenty-two years old, and Umeko was eighteen.

Charles Lanman, who with his wife had brought Umeko up like a daughter for ten years, escorted the pair as far as Chicago. In Chicago, Sutematsu and Umeko joined Professor J. D. Davis—who was on his way to Japan to take up a post at Doshisha University in Kyoto—and his wife for the remainder of the journey. Leaving Chicago by train, the group traveled through Omaha before stopping in Cheyenne, Wyoming, where Professor Davis had some business to attend to.

The news of the arrival of the two Japanese girls soon spread throughout the small town. Sutematsu was asked to speak, and the two were given generous coverage in the local papers. They were somewhat taken aback by all the fuss. In a letter to Alice, Sutematsu describes what happened in the town.

> I must tell you of a dreadful experience I went through in Cheyenne. As you know Mr. Davis was to speak about Japan in one of the churches and also Mrs. Davis. All the churches united and held their service at the Opera House in the evening when Mr. Davis was asked to speak. Of course I went. At the end of the service Mr. Sanders the minister of the Congregational Church announced that there was to be a Ladies Missionary Meeting the following afternoon at which Mrs. Davis was to speak of her personal work in Japan and that one of the Japanese young ladies was also expected to address the society. I was thunder struck. I never heard of such a thing. I thought it was impertinent of Mr. Sanders to speak in that way when he had not said anything to us at all. So we considered not to attend that meeting but the missionary Mrs. Davis came to me and asked me as a favor to her to say something at the meeting and as she was so urgent about it, I consented. I did not know what to say but Mrs. Davis suggested that I should speak of the summer of our coming to this country and also of what I expect to do on my return. I said only a few words for I was not prepared for such a thing at all, but the people were satisfied. Indeed we have been lionized since we came to Cheyenne. Actually a reporter came to interview us! Fortunately we were out so we escaped the ordeal. The people were very hospitable and warm hearted, but rather trying as they were rather inquisitive.
>
> (Wyoming, October 1882)

After eleven years in America, Sutematsu had grown from a docile Japanese girl into a woman able to speak her mind without hesitancy.

On October 31, Sutematsu and Umeko boarded the *Arabic* in San Francisco, their arms overflowing with flowers from well-wishers. Ships traveling to Japan in winter usually took a southern route, but the *Arabic's* captain had decided to go via the north, a route that was shorter by five hundred miles. From the first day out the Pacific belied its name, and strong winds and rain lashed the vessel. Even the purser, who was making his fifty-seventh Pacific crossing, told the passengers that he had never experienced such unrelenting storms.

Those on board could neither walk nor sit for much of the time, and as Sutematsu noted in her diary, at bedtime she was too busy clinging to the bunk trying to avoid being thrown out to contemplate sleep. All of her and Umeko's belongings fell out of their trunks, leaving nowhere for the two women to put their feet. From other cabins could be heard the frequent crash of plates falling to the floor. To Sutematsu and Umeko, clinging to their beds while fighting off hunger and seasickness, it must have seemed as if they had embarked on some kind of oceangoing hell. The seamen muttered among themselves that the inclement weather was caused by the presence of too many missionaries, which had incurred the wrath of the sea god. There were, in fact, an unusually large number of clergymen aboard: of the nineteen passengers only six, including Sutematsu and Umeko, were not of the cloth.

Despite the biting cold and her battle with seasickness, Sutematsu made a point of going up on deck to talk to the crew and to the dining room to spend time with the other passengers; she wanted to know what had been happening in Japan, and to practice the Japanese that she had faithfully studied during her stay in the United States, even during her busy days at Vassar. On calmer days, she took the opportunity to write to Alice, telling her about shipboard life and what she would need to bring on the voyage when she came to Japan.

To begin with I better tell you what you ought to do when you come over. First, if you come about this time bring all the warm clothes you possess, that is all your thick flannel and if you bring just an ulster better bring also a cardigan jacket; also a thick nubia, that is indispensable because a hat or a cap is not sufficient. You must have something warm to put right over your hat: a thick shawl and a rug to put over your knees when you sit on deck, a pair of overshoes; leggings might be useful as you have leg ache so much; Need not bring any books unless you choose, for there is a good library in this boat at least. . . . In the way of medicines, better bring brandy which is very good when taken in tea and strengthening during sea sickness: some sort of cathartic pills or something that will serve that purpose are very necessary. . . .

By the way I have found that it costs twenty-five dollars to take a dog on the steamer. The purser says that there is some disease which attacks all foreign dogs in Japan, but I will find out more particularly whether it is so. I think twenty-five is not a very large price considering all things though it is about half of what a steerage passenger pays.

(November 18, 1882)

As the voyage neared completion the weather improved. Bright sunny days followed one after the other and it was hard to believe the sea had ever been anything but kind. The ship made faster progress too, and Sutematsu and Umeko spent every day on deck, scanning the horizon for a glimpse of home.

Commemorative photo taken with Mrs. De Long in 1871, shortly before departing for the United States.

The Iwakura Mission From left: Takayoshi Kido, Naoyoshi Yamaguchi, Tomomi Iwakura, Hirobumi Ito, and Toshimichi Okubo.

From left: Shigeko Nagai, Teiko Ueda, Ryoko Yoshimasu, Umeko Tsuda, and Sutematsu Yamakawa, shortly after their arrival in Washington, 1872. (*Ishiguro Collection*)

The alumnae house of Vassar College, which at one time housed a "Princess Oyama Memorial Room," a reproduction of Sutematsu's dormitory room at the college.

The Bacon house. (*The New Haven Colony Historical Society Collection*)

Sutematsu as a student at Vassar College, around 1880.

Sutematsu as a student at Vassar College, at a Poughkeepsie photo studio.

Sutematsu's lifelong friend Alice Bacon.

Alice's mother, Katherine Bacon, and her father, Reverend Leonard Bacon, around 1870.

The Vassar College class of 1882. Class president and valedictorian Sutematsu is seated in the fourth row, fifth from left. (*Vassar Special Collections*)

Sutematsu as a Vassar graduate, at a New York photo studio in 1882.

Sutematsu in court robes, about to pay an obligatory visit to the Imperial Palace shortly after returning to Japan in 1883.

Iwao Oyama as a student in France, around 1872.

Sutematsu in her finery, about to attend a ball at the Rokumeikan, around 1888.

The Rokumeikan. (*Kasumi Kaikan*)

Dance lessons at the Rokumeikan. (*Ukiyo-e by Tadasu Watanabe, Watanabe Woodblock Art Gallery*)

Commemorative photo of the Meiji Emperor's visit to the newly built Oyama family house in Tokyo in 1890.

Sutematsu holding her first son, around 1886.

Sutematsu with Alice Bacon during her visit to Japan to help establish the Joshi Eigakujuku (English school for girls), in 1900. From left: Umeko, Alice, Shigeko, and Sutematsu.

A Japanese-made silk photo stand showing the Oyamas, found in the home of Alfred Bacon, Alice's nephew.

Sutematsu around 1900 (forty years old).

During the Russo-Japanese War, 1905: An article in the *The World Magazine* describing Sutematsu's and Shigeko's activities for the war cause.

At the home of Chiharu Watanabe (Sutematsu's son-in-law) in Kojimachi, Tokyo around 1890: From front, second from left: Sutematsu's fourth daughter, Hisako; fourth from left: Tomeko Watanabe (the author's grandmother), holding her first son. Sutematsu is fifth from left. Back row, third from left: Chiharu Watanabe (the author's grandfather); sixth from left: Iwao Oyama.

Iwao Oyama's departure to the continent during the Russo-Japanese War, 1904. From left: Sutematsu; her eldest son, Takashi; Iwao Oyama; their second son, Kashiwa; and their fourth daughter, Hisako.

The Oyama couple in later years.

Days of Disappointment

RETURNING TO FAMILY

On November 21, 1882 the *Arabic* sailed into Yokohama under clear blue skies, two days behind schedule. It was the first time Sutematsu and Umeko had seen their homeland in eleven years, since they had left its shores with the Iwakura Mission on December 23, 1871. Sutematsu later described their excitement on seeing Japan after so long.

I could not sleep the night before our arrival: neither could my friend Ume, who occupied the same state-room with me, so we talked till the small hours of the night, when we were able to doze a little and get some rest before the excitement of the day should begin. Hardly had we slept an hour or two, when we were aroused by some one shouting into our room: "Land!" Up we jumped, and, dressing hastily, we ran for the deck. Yes, there it was! We could descry distinctly the outline of a mountain range in the misty distance.

It seemed days and weeks from the time when we first saw land to the time when we entered the Bay of Yedo, though in reality it was about five hours. . . . Soon our steamer ceased to move, and small tugs from the hotels, private boats, and small craft of all kinds came to meet the "*Arabic*," to take the passengers and the baggage ashore. I did not expect any one to meet me, on account of the great uncertainty in regard to the time of the steamer's arrival. What was my joy, then, when Ume's sharp eyes discovered a small tug, whose occupants were waving handkerchiefs and seemed to be frantic with excitement. I knew then that my friends were in the boat. Nearer and nearer it approached the steamer, and we found that the party consisted of Ume's father and sister; Mr. Takahashi, our former consul in New York; my two sisters; and Shige, a great friend of Ume's and mine, who had been with us for ten years in America. It was all so strange and bewildering that I felt as if I were in a dream. . . .
(*Independent*, April 1883)

With hardly a chance to talk to the relatives who had come to welcome her, Sutematsu was whisked away in a jinrikisha with Shigeko, and while being bounced about in what seemed an alarming fashion the two women caught up on each other's news. Riding down the narrow streets with houses tightly crammed on either side, Sutematsu felt, as she recalled later, "as if I were visiting Lilliput."

In Yokohama the party stopped at the residence of former consul Takahashi for lunch. Asked by the consul's wife whether they preferred Western or Japanese cooking, Sutematsu and Umeko replied that of course they would like to taste the food of their home country.

As Mrs. Takahashi's carefully prepared lunch was served, all eyes turned on the two young women. Had they forgotten how to use chopsticks? everyone wondered. Sutematsu wrote later: ". . . great was their surprise when I ate the lunch as naturally as one who has never left the soil of the Mikado's empire. Even Ume, who had completely forgotten her native tongue, was at home with these implements. It is a strange fact that the use of the chopsticks seems to be inherited and the last thing to be forgotten by Japanese otherwise denationalized."

After resting a while at the Takahashis', Sutematsu and Umeko walked to Yokohama Station and boarded a train for Tokyo. The line between Shinbashi in Tokyo and Yokohama had not been completed until a year after they left, so it was in fact their first train ride in Japan. An hour later they arrived in Tokyo, and after another hour of being tossed about in a jinrikisha, Sutematsu arrived at her mother's home in Ushigome. By that time it was evening.

At the gate Sutematsu's mother, her brother Kenjiro and his wife Riu, her sister Tokiwa and her husband and son, three students, and four servants were waiting. Sutematsu had imagined this scene a hundred times over in the past weeks. So, no doubt, had Ioi, her mother, and the day had finally arrived. The girl she had sent off to America, without knowing whether she would ever see her again, had spent eleven years in the service of her country and had returned as a beautiful young woman.

Not everyone was glad to see the long-lost Sutematsu. Tokiwa's son Shigeharu took one look at his aunt and burst into tears. Surprised, Sutematsu stepped forward to comfort him, but that only made things worse and the little boy's howling increased in volume. With her strange kimono, the likes of which he had never seen, and equally strange hairdo, "Auntie Sutematsu"'s sudden appearance had given her young nephew a fright. Not only that, but his grandmother, who always fussed over him more than anyone else in the family did, was quite oblivious to him today and had eyes only for Sutematsu. For quite some time after their initial encounter, Shigeharu continued to be afraid of Sutematsu in her Western clothes, and it was only when she began to wear a kimono like "all the other aunties" that he was able to accept her.

The Yamakawas took great care of Sutematsu on her return home: they bought Western furniture because she found it difficult to sit on the floor, kept the fire stoked at all times to prevent her catching a cold from the Japanese climate, and agonized over what to cook. She felt as if she were a guest, not a member of the family: ". . . my brother is very considerate and kind and does everything to make me comfortable. So are all the rest of the family. They all devote themselves to me and I am in a fair way to become spoilt."

"As to the language," she wrote to Alice, "I had forgotten it almost entirely, so that I supposed I would find myself very awkwardly situated when I returned home, but to my surprise, as soon as I touched my native soil, my tongue seemed to be loosened as it were, and though I spoke bad Japanese, I could make all my wants known and converse with my family very easily." She was grateful to Kenjiro for being such a hard taskmaster all those years. She also soon relearned how to properly wear a kimono.

> I like the Japanese dress very much and have worn it in the house ever since I came. I think I shall always wear it at home; but, since I have not yet learned to wear it gracefully and naturally, for a while yet I shall wear foreign dress when going out, though by so doing I make myself a conspicuous object, for there are very few European or American ladies in Tokio and only about a half-dozen Japanese ladies here have adopted the foreign dress. The Japanese dress is very pretty and graceful, and, when worn with good taste, European costume cannot rival it in beauty. One reason why I cannot wear Japanese dress out of doors is that I cannot bring myself to arrange my hair in true Japanese fashion, a fashion which, though beautiful in appearance, requires so much pomatum for its proper carrying out that the very thought of it is repulsive to one who has been accustomed to European coiffure. Then, again,

Japanese ladies do not arrange their hair oftener than once in two or three days, and I never could sleep on the wooden pillow which this infrequent hair-dressing renders necessary or without letting my hair down at night.
(*Independent*, April 1883)

Sutematsu soon realized that her family's circumstances were far better than during the days of the wasteland of Tonami. The eldest son Hiroshi had served with distinction during the Saga Rebellion and been promoted to major general, achieving far more than any other member of the former Aizu domain. Kenjiro was a professor in the science department of the University of Tokyo, and older sisters Futaba and Misao were independently pursuing their own careers: Futaba as a dormitory superintendent at the Tokyo Women's Normal School, and Misao working as an interpreter and living with a French family after studying for several years in Russia.

Despite the fact that all the members of the Yamakawa family were fortunate enough to be in relatively well-paying jobs, there were, however, still others to support, such as students, and day-to-day life was not particularly comfortable. Sutematsu described the situation to Alice in her first letter after returning home.

My brother (I mean my younger brother) has a very good position and gets a good salary for a Japanese but the trouble is he has so many to support that he has to scrimp himself to make others comfortable. Ever since the war the Aidzu people have become very poor and all our relatives have to be helped more or less. There are about twenty people to whom my two brothers send money besides supporting their immediate relatives and besides educating and supporting two to five students all the time. At present there are only three students in this house and though feeding and clothing and education of them are not very expensive, still when there are three or four in the house all the time it is one source of expense to a large family.

(December 11, 1882)

The more care and attention Sutematsu received at home, and the more she enjoyed the warmth of family after so many years apart, the sooner she felt she ought to change her situation and somehow lighten the burden for others.

JOB-HUNTING

Soon after her return, Sutematsu headed for the Ministry of Education to formally report her arrival in Japan and to discuss possible employment prospects. The Hokkaido Development Bureau, which had recruited the girls to study in America with such fanfare, had since been dissolved, and Sutematsu and her fellow students were now under the jurisdiction of the Ministry of Education. Having been exhorted by the empress when she left to work hard and return as a role model for the women of her country, naturally Sutematsu expected that her country would have work for her.

Unfortunately, that was not the case. Despite the fact that universities and government departments virtually snapped up male students returning from overseas as soon as they stepped off the boat and automatically guaranteed them membership in the nation's elite, the government had no plans for Sutematsu and Umeko. And after ten years of education in America, they were hardly going to be content with the role of "intelligent mother" that Kiyotaka Kuroda and Arinori Mori had envisaged for them years earlier. Sutematsu expressed her exasperation in a letter to Alice:

In the first place you must know that Japanese do not regard time as anything valuable. In consequence of this peculiar idea it is next to impossibility to get anything done in hurry. Now

you may imagine how anxious I am to get to work immediately, but as yet the Educational Department has taken hardly
any notice of my return and I am waiting for some communication from it. I am not likely to have any work to do before
next spring.

(December 11, 1882)

Sutematsu did not relish waiting for the unenthusiastic Ministry
of Education to find work for her, but on the other hand, she
could not depend on her family for the capital necessary to finance
a new business. She decided to ask Alice:

I do not want to waste my time and . . . I need ready money.
So I think of leaving this home as soon as convenient and
with my eldest sister who is sort of a preceptress at the Normal School take a little house in some convenient place where
people can have a little more access to than here and have a
few private pupils from the higher classes of people. I mean:
to have young wives of officers or daimios daughters who
can't go to school. I do not believe I can have more than four
of five but even with that beginning I hope to increase the
number till it becomes a regular school. I had a long talk with
Mr. Uriu (Shige's husband) and he seems to be pretty confident that I shall succeed. Now in order to take a house we
need everything from kitchen utensils to parlor ornaments.
Though we think of having only a parlor, one bed-room, a
kitchen and a little place for the maid to sleep in, and though
Japanese house keeping is very simple, still there are a few
things necessary for even such a house. And in order to get
them we need all of a hundred dollars and what I am going to
do is to ask you if it is possible for you to lend me a hundred
dollars. I can not return it soon or at once but could you do
it? It is not yet decided that we shall do it for we have not yet
even consulted my brother but in case such a plan is carried

out, could you lend us an assistance in that direction.

(December 11, 1882)

Kenjiro vetoed this scheme of Sutematsu's, arguing that if the Ministry of Education did not come up with a job for her by spring, the government should create one for her. Until then, he told his sister, it would be better not to start work of any other kind. Still wanting to ease the financial burden on the family, Sutematsu hit upon the idea of putting her first impressions of Japan down on paper, for publication in an American newspaper or magazine. She asked Alice to find a publisher; her article "First Impressions of Japan," written two weeks after her return, was published in the *Independent*, a leading religious newspaper, in April 1883.

The truth of the matter was, the Ministry of Education really did not have a clue about what to do with the two young women who repeatedly pressed it for work. Sutematsu, with her degree from Vassar College, was no less well qualified than any of the male returnees, and better qualified than some, but because of her sex, officials of the Ministry of Education were reluctant to give her a university teaching post. There was no precedent. It was also suggested that Sutematsu's intelligence and linguistic ability be utilized to assist foundering treaty negotiations—not surprisingly, nothing came of that suggestion either.

However, the intransigence of the Ministry of Education and of Japanese society in general concerning the employment of females was not the only problem. Sutematsu and Umeko were seriously disadvantaged by their inability to read or write in Japanese. Sutematsu was able to carry on everyday conversation, thanks to her contact with Shigeko and Kenjiro, but Umeko had completely forgotten how to speak, since she had not used Japanese at all during her ten years in the Lanman household, and she was unable to converse with her family at even the most basic level when she returned to Japan. Japanese society at the time had no place for a

Japanese, particularly a woman, who was unable to use its own language.

Sutematsu, Shigeko, and Umeko never mastered Japanese, and throughout their lives wrote letters in English and preferred to read English newspapers. My grandmother would recall that when Shigeko and Umeko came for a visit, "Mother would speak to them excitedly in English, and they would play cards. She was always most animated when speaking English." On another occasion when she was a child, my grandmother walked into Sutematsu's room late at night, to find her hurriedly covering sheets of paper on the desk. When she asked her mother what she was doing Sutematsu snapped at her, "It's writing practice. I'm too embarrassed to do it in front of you all, so I wait until everyone's gone to bed."

In September 1872, a year after Sutematsu left for the United States, the first Education Order was promulgated, and for the first time education for females was formally acknowledged to be desirable. The new laws proclaimed they would "do away with the evil of women's illiteracy" and "make it compulsory for boys and girls to attend elementary school," and were designed to be carried out in a spirit of equality between the sexes.

The reality was different. The deeply rooted idea that wise mothers brought up clever children was still the strongest influence on the curriculum, and subjects such as handcrafts and sewing were considered the most important for girls, a far cry from any concept of educating females as individuals and encouraging them to aim for personal success.

The first Education Order was replaced by another in 1878, one more moralistic in nature and based on Confucian ideas. Women were to be obedient and chaste, and were only valued in relation to parents, husband, and sons. An elementary school textbook on ethics stated, "If a woman gives up her life inside the home and goes out to occupy herself with other matters, the effect on society is disastrous." Not much support here for the advancement of women. In fact, the new education law served to place even more pressure on women to stay shut inside their homes than they had previously felt.

Only half of Japanese children attended elementary school at that time, and of those who did, only a small percentage were girls. Higher education for women barely existed, and was confined to a handful of public girls' schools and mission schools.

So it was that Sutematsu and Umeko returned to a Japan still not wrested out of the feudal era. Despite being the first Japanese women to study in America and coming home with dreams of helping the cause of women's education, the only work the two could conceivably engage in, as unmarried women of their class, was private English tutoring: and the remuneration for that was so low that any fees gained would be used up paying for jinrikisha to travel to and from the homes of pupils.

AN OASIS

Amidst disappointment and frustration, the place where Sutematsu and Umeko felt most at ease following their return to Japan was at the home of Shigeko and her husband, Sotokichi Uryu. Shigeko had waited until her friends came back before getting married. Since the Uryu home was located midway between those of Sutematsu and Umeko, it became a natural meeting place. Another advantage was that Sotokichi worked for the Naval Office and was frequently away, and that enabled Sutematsu and Umeko to stay with Shigeko.

The main attraction of Shigeko's home, however, was that it served as a nucleus to which students returning from overseas gravitated to exchange experiences and views. Both husband and wife had lived in America, they had no children yet, nor were they living with elderly parents, so their home was ideal as a gathering place.

I go to Shige's frequently; in fact I spend half the time there.

Whenever I am invited out to any place I generally come back to her house and spend the night because my home is so far away from everybody. The last two weeks have been quite gay and I have been at Shige's most of the time. Shige's house is very convenient and as there is no body but herself and Mr. Uriu I feel perfectly at home there. She gathers a small party of young people around her so that her company are about our age. She invites young men who have been abroad and who are consequently more congenial than those who never have seen other countries. Most of them are unmarried and are professors at the University or else hold some important position under the government.

(January 8, 1883)

Sutematsu took her brother's advice and put her plan for a school on hold until spring. In any case, she knew that to start any sort of work she would need to improve her Japanese, so in between private English teaching she persevered in being tutored in her native language, undergoing three intense sessions a week.

What spare time Sutematsu had was spent mainly at Shigeko's, where she found an outlet for her frustration by talking with the people who met there. Reasoning that such a gathering was meaningless without some specific aim, she formed a private club modelled on "Our Society" in New Haven. The purpose of the group was to work toward the spread of English and of Western customs and culture, and to apply new moral concepts to Japanese society. The carefully selected members would get together once a month, taking turns holding meetings in their homes. The first meeting was scheduled for January 11, 1883. Home scarcely two months, Sutematsu was already trying to transplant her American experiences onto Japanese society.

The 1883 New Year's celebration was an especially happy one for the Yamakawas, with their long-lost daughter finally home, but as the festivities tailed off, the question of Sutematsu's marriage began to loom large in the minds of family members. At a time when most girls were married by the age of sixteen, in the eyes of most Sutematsu was truly an old maid. Relatives and friends of the family began to approach her with what they considered good matches.

> Oh, Alice, I don't know what to do. It is perplexing this life. It is nothing but a perpetual struggle after some thing. If it is not for one thing, it is for another. What would you say if I were engaged? But never fear. I have so far refused to marry three distinct persons and perhaps I may not have another chance even if I were willing. One I might have married for position and money but I resisted the temptation. He will be they say one of the ministers to Europe one of these days. The others—well I suppose I might have married for love, for yet neither of them had money or rank—but I didn't. So when you come to Japan you will still find me an old maid. Do you know Alice that girls who are above twenty are old maids? I am one and mother says that I may not have another offer.
>
> (January 16, 1883)

In the United States, Sutematsu had interacted with well-educated women who were independent and in control of their own lives, so she felt extremely impatient with the Japanese system whereby a woman was not considered a responsible member of society until she married. Especially annoying was the fact that even men who had been overseas for some years and returned to become leading members of Japanese society still preferred to marry young girls with no ideas or opinions of their own.

> I think that is the one reason why men can not be good. How can girls of seventeen or eighteen keep their husbands straight? I am sure I don't know what is going to become of Japan.
>
> (January 16, 1883)

Sutematsu also felt discouraged by what she saw as a complete lack of morals in her fellow countrymen, not surprising considering that she had lived with a deeply religious family in a town where the Puritan tradition still had great influence.

> I suppose you will be shocked if you hear some of the things I do on Sunday. But I think even your strictness will change when you come to Japan though you are not a Japanese and for a Japanese it is impossible to observe the Sabbath as it is done in America. You can not imagine how bad people can be and when you hear so much that is wicked going on, the breaking of Sabbath seems no sin at all. I have often given up the idea of trying to improve the present state of society for the work to be accomplished is simply enormous, and it does seem as if the influence of one or two women can hardly be felt. Drunkenness is very common among men and not more than one in a hundred who live a good, pure life. I am sure I can count on my fingers those who live blamelessly.
>
> (January 8, 1883)

PORTIA'S LOVE

Partly as a distraction from her disappointment with Japanese society, Sutematsu decided to use the experience she had gained in the Shakespeare Club at Vassar to perform plays in English with members of her newly formed private club. As she explained to Alice, the aims were to give Japanese a chance to improve their English, and to provide some moral education. The works chosen all contained an important moral or two in the story line, which Sutematsu hoped would serve to enlighten her compatriots in some way. The membership consisted of Sutematsu, Shigeko, Umeko, the wife of the principal of Tokyo Normal School, Shigeko's husband Sotokichi, Naibu Kanda (professor of English at the University of Tokyo), Keikichi Mitsukuri and Joji Sakurai of the same university's science department, Shigeko's brother Eisaku Masuda, and a few others from time to time.

The club had hardly formed when its members received a request to put on a play—from Shigeko's elder brother Takashi Masuda, president of the Mitsui trading company. (Soon after she was born Shigeko had been adopted by the Nagai family, of samurai origins from Shizuoka Prefecture, and so had used the name of Nagai before she was married.) Takashi was knowledgeable about the West, having at the age of fifteen joined his father on a mission to Europe, and it was he who advised Shigeko to go to America. A well-known figure in both business and politics, he owned a luxurious home in the Shinagawa area of Tokyo and was often mentioned in Sutematsu's letters to Alice as "Shigeko's rich brother." Sutematsu, Shigeko, and Umeko frequently visited the Masuda home and enjoyed playing tennis there, which at the time was still a rare pastime in Japan.

Masuda requested that an English play be performed at Shigeko's wedding reception, to which he planned to invite leading figures in politics and the business community.

> As I told you we are getting up a play. We intended to act a farce but when we were discussing the plan Shige's brother heard it and was very anxious to have it done at his house on the occasion of a party to be given for Shige: so, as we did not have but ten days, we gave up our original play and took the last two acts of "The Merchant of Venice". We hope to do the other leisurely some time. The play will come off tomorrow night and I am very busy. Can you imagine me as Portia? Mr. Uryu is Antonio, Mr. Kanda Bassanio, Ume Nerissa, etc. etc. At the trial scene I am to wear my fur cloak, a velvet cap and a black dress. In the next act I shall wear my commencement dress. The gentlemen's costumes are very good as they have borrowed them from a lady who had the play at her house. Shylock's part is splendidly taken by Shige's younger

brother who is I think the best amateur performer I ever saw. (He really has a splendid dramatic talent. He has seen the play so much that he knows exactly what to do.) The party will be a large affair and all sorts of swell people will come to it. But since half of them won't understand English we have no fear of stage fright at all.

(January 24, 1883)

The day of the reception arrived, and the Masuda mansion was packed with the ladies and gentlemen of Tokyo's high society, dazzling in their best finery. The first English performance of *The Merchant of Venice* in Japan would take place that day, and the crowd buzzed with anticipation. In addition, it was said, the performers were all members of that exclusive group of intellectuals who had recently returned from overseas. Judging by the conversations of those at the reception, the play threatened to overshadow the real stars, the bride, Shigeko, and her groom, Sotokichi.

Sutematsu in the role of Portia became the star attraction that day. Her height and un-Japanese appearance, ease of movement in her fitting Western dress, and dramatic condemnation of Shylock in perfect English stole the show completely. The club's first performance was a resounding success.

Despite carrying off such a triumph, it appears that Sutematsu had been troubled throughout the rehearsals. She first mentions this to Alice in a letter dated January 28, probably written after the performance, when she had time for other matters again. Whatever was troubling her was obviously of a very personal nature, for in her letter Sutematsu shys away from saying anything specific about it.

What a trouble it is to live! This world is nothing but full of cares. I have got into most horrible trouble and I don't know what to do. You are my only comfort for I can write to you and let off my feelings. I can't talk to even Shige for with her began the trouble and I am afraid we will have no end of row. I need not tell you the nature of the trouble for it is sufficient to say I am in it. The people at home of course know it but I can not have so much sympathy from them. But never mind. I hope it will all come right in the end.

(January 28, 1883)

An unusually hesitant and inarticulate letter for Sutematsu. Three weeks later, she finally had the courage to tell all.

Do you recollect that I told you in one of my letters that I had an offer from a young man? Well, he has given me no end of trouble and I have been worried to death about it. When he wrote to me, I was going to refuse him right off but both Mother and Shige were very anxious that I should consider the matter, so I told him to wait for me five or six months. I said I could not tell whether I would say yes or no and if he did not want to wait so long with an uncertainty before him, he may consider my answer as no. He said he would wait. So we met very often and were very good friends. Of course it was very pleasant to have a young handsome man very attentive to you and to have him think your slightest wish is as a law. He is very good looking and only 26. He speaks the best English of anyone I ever saw in Japan perhaps excepting Ume and is a teacher of English at the University. Moreover he is a very good Christian and he is thoroughly good. It is all very nice and pleasant to have him make love but that kind of thing could not go on forever. I feel I ought put stop to it if I did not intend to marry him. I did have serious thoughts of saying yes for I liked him very much and he was in dead earnest. But when I thought of it more, I did not think it would be best, for one thing he is very young and boyish.

(February 20, 1883)

Barely home three months, Sutematsu had already attracted her first real suitor. We have no way of knowing whether Sutematsu had such feelings during her stay in America, but knowing how rational and self-disciplined she was, it is probable she would have felt the responsibility of being a government scholarship recipient too heavily to become involved in any way with the opposite sex. It is reasonable, therefore, to presume that the subject of the letter was the first man Sutematsu had ever seriously considered marrying.

Having finally determined that marriage to him would not be right for her, Sutematsu wrote a letter to the young man, asking him to forget all that had passed between them. Undeterred by her refusal, he turned up at the Yamakawa home unexpectedly one day to talk things over, prompting Sutematsu to hide in her room and send one of the servants to the door, with the excuse that she had a heavy cold and could not possibly see him. Still not one to give up, he went directly to Sutematsu's sister Futaba at the Tokyo Women's Normal School and begged her to arrange a meeting. Feeling sorry for the lovesick young man, Futaba did all in her power to persuade Sutematsu to reconsider, but to no avail. Sutematsu was firm in her resolve.

Some time later, Sutematsu received a long letter from her former suitor. In her own words, the letter "seems more like a curse than any thing else." She deeply regretted not refusing his proposal immediately, instead of causing him such pain. Since the man was a close friend of Shigeko's husband, Sotokichi, and came to every gathering held at the Uryu home, Sutematsu avoided her friend's house in dread of meeting him; however, it is doubtful whether she was able to avoid him altogether, especially since members of the upper classes at that time moved in a very restricted circle.

> I wonder if you think as I do that the happiest period of one's life is one's childhood. I feel more than ever the heavy responsibility of my future and present—life, too and wish those careless days at Vassar could come back again. Oh Alice what a tangle this life is! I never used to think much of the

dark side of life and used to feel so confident of future and of own strength but now I am not certain of either. . . . I suppose I feel a little more blue lately because I have done something which I feel as if I might have done otherwise. You know I wrote to you in my last letter about that poor young man. I had then no idea that it was as anything so serious, but I am afraid I have saddened his whole life. I am so sorry for him and I feel that perhaps I might not to have refused him. I have met him since, and he has changed completely. He looks so sad and melancholy as if he did not care what became of him. I suppose he will get over it soon for men do forget such things in a wonderfully short time, but just at present it goes very hard with him. A few days ago I met him at a party— that was the second time I met him since I wrote him my last letter, and before; he was so different from what he used to be at a dance.

(March 18, 1883)

My heart went out to Sutematsu the first time I read these troubled letters. Out of the huge bundle she wrote to Alice Bacon over a forty-year period, they stood out. Suddenly I felt closer to her than ever before; I empathized with her romantic dilemma, but more importantly, she seemed more human and vulnerable— not always the stable, rational spirit she appeared to be. Sutematsu's marriage to Iwao Oyama had never seemed quite right to me: I had always felt that, labelled as "one of the first Japanese women to study overseas," she had married him out of feelings of obligation toward her country. After all, what attraction could a man eighteen years her senior—with average looks and three daughters in tow— have for a young woman? After reading of Sutematsu's ill-starred love affair, I felt my suspicions confirmed—she herself saw the problem of her marriage as a public affair, superseding any private feelings she may have had. It is thus unlikely that what she saw as her suitor's lack of maturity was the major factor in her decision not to marry him. A voice inside had reminded her that if she were to wed, it would have to be a marriage that enabled her to fulfill her responsibilities and obligations as a first female government student to study abroad, not one that she entered into merely for love. If Sutematsu had not been carrying the heavy burden of her position, in all probability she would have married her young and handsome suitor.

THE MYSTERY SUITOR

So who was the unfortunate young man? She referred to him merely as "he" throughout, not even giving away his identity to Alice. Was it Sutematsu's way of protecting him—or herself—from embarrassment?

There are a few clues: he was twenty-six, handsome, the second-best English speaker in Japan after Umeko, an English teacher at a university, a Christian, and a friend of Sotokichi Uryu. He was probably among the guests at those gatherings in the Uryu home. If his English was as good as Sutematsu says, he must have spent considerable time abroad. A close friend of Sotokichi (who had attended the U.S. Naval Academy at Annapolis), we can presume that they were in America at about the same time, and that he was among those who had studied in the United States at the beginning of the Meiji period, along with Sutematsu and the other girls.

Among the vast amount of material I had gathered for my research was a small pamphlet with the title *The Rutgers College Graduates in Japan*, by William Griffis. (Griffis had been invited to Japan as a science teacher by the Fukui domain at the beginning of the Meiji period.)

The pamphlet contained a list of some of the Japanese students who had attended Rutgers, or who had lived in the town of New Brunswick over the twenty-year period from the end of the Tokugawa shogunate to about midway through the Meiji period. I was less than optimistic about finding a name with details that matched those of Sutematsu's young man. Leafing through the pages, I stopped short at the name "Naibu Kanda." Kanda was a name that had often appeared in Sutematsu's letters. Eagerly I read on. "The son of an eminent progressive Liberal in Tokio, whom the writer knew, came to the United States at the age of fourteen. After six months' stay with Dr. Corwin, he went to Amherst College, graduating in full course, spending altogether five or six years in this country. He is one of the best speakers in English in Japan, a prominent Christian, and has been very active in the general work of uniting the two civilizations."

Certain I had found my man, I remembered that, according to Sutematsu's letters, a Mr. Kanda had played the part of Bassanio in *The Merchant of Venice* that night of January 25, 1883. To prepare a performance in only ten days requires a great deal of intense practice, and it is not difficult to imagine that such an experience could have drawn those two young people together very quickly.

Mr. Kanda was without a doubt one of the leading lights of Japanese education. Furthermore, a passage in the book *Ishin no ryugakusei* (Students Who Studied Abroad during the Meiji Restoration Period) by Kenichi Kamigaito reads, "Umeko had many proposals, including one from Naibu Kanda, a famous English scholar of the period. She turned down his proposal, however, saying, 'It was thanks to my country that I was able to study overseas, so until I return that favor I cannot possibly get married.'"

This account is confirmed by comments that Sutematsu made in one of her letters to Alice.

> By the way to continue that episode of mine, I must tell you how that young man is getting along. It is scarcely two months but as I said he has got over it wonderfully well. I have met him lots of times and he has returned to the normal state of mind. So now I feel no uncomfortable sensation in talking to him. We are planning to have his thoughts turn to Ume and the other day a hint to that effect was given to him and he does not refuse to take it absolutely. I think it will be a

good thing for both sides if they only see it in that light themselves. He is a thoroughly good young man—in fact he is the only one of my acquaintances who can be said to be good. By good I do not mean he is the only one who is moral but he is thoroughly unselfish and amiable to such a degree that people take often an unfair advantage of him. He is not at all badly off and Ume would never suffer if she married him. I hope it will be successful but very often these things do not turn out as we expect.

(April 12, 1883)

THE DECISION TO MARRY

While Sutematsu was in the midst of her problems with Naibu Kanda, a notice finally arrived from the Ministry of Education indicating that work had been found for her. A teacher of biology and physiology at the Tokyo Women's Normal School was about to leave, and Sutematsu was invited to take his place. Physiology had been Sutematsu's best subject at Vassar, so she was thrilled at the news. Moreover the salary was an incredible fifty yen per month. At the time Shigeko was earning thirty yen a month teaching at the Tokyo Music School, and was said to be the highest-earning woman in the country. If Sutematsu could combine this new job with her private English tutoring, the school she was planning with Alice might become more than a dream.

There was only one problem: the Ministry of Education proceeded to inform Sutematsu that she had to take up the post within two weeks, ignorant and insensitive of the fact that as a returnee, she could no longer speak her native language fluently. Disappointed, she turned the job down. Although her everyday conversation had progressed a great deal, Sutematsu's reading and writing ability in Japanese was still at elementary school level, and there was no way she could teach from Japanese textbooks or write in Japanese on a blackboard.

What had her ten years in America been for? Sutematsu had

returned to Japan resolving to spend her life in the service of her country, but without the ability to read and write Japanese it seemed there was no use for her talents. To make matters worse, even with a career, as a single Japanese woman she had no hope of being taken seriously. There seemed to be no mercy for the unmarried woman in a still-feudalistic society, where Confucian doctrines had an enormous influence on the prescribed behavior for women.

> Oh, Alice my views on various subjects change so rapidly. I see now the necessity for Japanese women to be married. It is very different from America—this question of marriage. You can not tell till you have been in Japan and be a Japanese, but really it is necessary. I don't know but I shall have to come to the matrimonial state myself. . . .
>
> (February 20, 1883)

Paradoxically, once the "Kanda problem" had been resolved, Sutematsu reappraised her dream of building a school and began to think seriously about marriage.

> People talk of dying for one's country as a glorious thing, but to me, to live for one's country seems infinitely more self-sac-rificing. If it is possible that by the death of someone Japan could be benefited in some way I would willingly, rather gladly be that one, but that is impossible. What Japan needs is the life-long services of those who have her interest most at heart.
>
> (March 19, 1883)

Home barely four months, Sutematsu was already having to make a decision that would affect the rest of her life. Marriage or career? The pressures Sutematsu faced from family members as well as society in general put her in a quandary. She observed that being single was a handicap. It made it difficult for a woman to be respected and have any significant influence in society.

Sutematsu wrote in one of her letters: "Of the three of us, Shige is the happiest." Shigeko, who had completed her studies, come home, and married, was indeed happy in her life with Soto-kichi, and was also lucky enough to work as a music teacher, an occupation in which her lack of Japanese ability made little difference. Umeko had just turned nineteen and was not yet quite in danger of being labelled an old maid. Sutematsu saw herself as the most troubled of the three, and after mulling over the problem decided that if she had to live in Japan and do things the Japanese way, she must take the plunge and marry in the hope that once she had, she could do something for the country.

As Sutematsu was wavering over making a decision, she received a well-timed proposal.

> By the way do you remember I told you that I had an offer from a gentle man in a rather high position. Well, he has asked me again and I am thinking of it. I do not know what is the best. . . . There does not seem to be any position that I can fill and the mere teaching is not what Japan needs most. What must be done is a change in the existing state of society and this can only be accomplished by married women. I mean that I do not think that teaching is the only way to benefit Japan. If I thought that if I did not teach, I would be perfectly useless to Japan, I would not hesitate to devote my whole life to teaching, but I feel sure that I can do some service to the country by giving up my pet plan. Of course, I would not marry either just because I can do more good, but I am considering this subject not only for Japan's account but also on my own. It would not be right to make myself perfectly miserable just because I think I can do some good but it is possible that I may be happier and at the same time become more useful. Some times I get so troubled for I do not know what

would be for the best. It is all so strange and confusing and I cannot tell what is right or what is wrong.

(April 5, 1883)

THE MINISTER OF WAR

The man who proposed to Sutematsu was none other than Iwao Oyama, minister of war, aged forty-two. Oyama was eighteen years older than Sutematsu and had three daughters, the oldest aged seven, by his previous wife Sawako, who had died in August the year before.

Oyama was born in Kajiyacho, the castle town of the Satsuma domain (present-day Kagoshima Prefecture) on October 10, 1842. He was the second son of samurai Hikohachi Tsunamasa Oyama.

Early on the morning of December 24, 1871, the sturdy twenty-nine-year-old Oyama, looking very much at home in his Western suit, stood on the deck of a French mail boat as it pulled away from Yokohama. Yokohama was quiet on that day, unlike the previous one, when the port had been the scene of a grand farewell for the hundred or so members of the Iwakura Mission, the first sent to the United States and Europe by the new Meiji government. Among those who had left, of course, had been the young Sutematsu Yamakawa. Both preoccupied with the tasks that lay before them and their duty to the new Japan, they sailed off to the "West," one across the Pacific and the other toward the Indian Ocean.

Major General Oyama, as he was then called, was off to France to study the modern weaponry of Europe. He intended to return with knowledge that would enable Japan to catch up with the West in that area. Oyama had been interested in weapons since his youth. He had been in command of the Satsuma First Artillery Company during the Hakodate War and had invented the "Yasuke cannon," a type of mortar named after his childhood appelation. The year before his journey to France, the new government had sent him on a tour of Europe and America as part of a mission assigned to observe combat events during the Franco-Prussian War. Witnessing the power of the French and Prussian weaponry firsthand, the group realized that Japan's own defenses were woefully inadequate. It concluded that the nation must begin manufacturing its own weapons rather than relying on imports from overseas.

After the mission's return, Oyama continued to feel strongly that Japan needed its own arms industry and, six months later, arranged to spend some time in France to study weaponry.

A month after arriving in Paris, Oyama decided there were too many Japanese in that city for his French to improve and shifted to Geneva, where he boarded with a Swiss family and absorbed himself in studying the language, which he eventually mastered. Between his studies he found time to visit armaments factories and military academies throughout Europe, as well as gain some understanding of European cultures.

Oyama had left for Europe intending to stay for ten years, but the political situation in Japan would not allow such indulgence. In the early years after the Meiji Restoration, Japan was thrown into chaos by antigovernment elements dissatisfied with the prefectural system, conscription, laws demanding that former samurai do away with their traditional top-knot hairstyle and relinquish their swords, the adoption of the Western calendar, and a host of other Westernizing and modernizing measures introduced by the Meiji leaders. The government itself was divided by the Korean issue. One faction argued that Japan should take over Korea before European powers, such as Britain, Russia, and France, pushed through China and Manchuria and used the Korean peninsula as a springboard for invading Japan. Takamori Saigo, Oyama's cousin and an important figure of the Meiji Restoration, was a leading advocate of such a move.

Saigo found himself opposed, however, by Tomomi Iwakura, Takayoshi Kido, and Toshimichi Okubo, on their return in September 1873 from the two-year Iwakura Mission. Now was not the time for fighting in Korea, they argued: their overseas experiences had shown them that Japan's priority should be building up its strength internally. The government and the emperor took note of what Iwakura and his colleagues had to say, and on October 24 an imperial rescript opposing invasion was issued. The defeated Saigo promptly announced his resignation, citing illness, and withdrew to his Kagoshima home. He was soon followed by his supporters, and there were angry rumblings from the military, who revered Saigo. The whole situation was a tinderbox threatening to ignite at any moment. After due consideration the government decided that the best way to deal with the crisis was to recall Saigo to Tokyo and give him a cabinet post, but someone whom Saigo trusted was needed to tackle the job of persuading him to play along. That someone ended up being an unwitting Iwao Oyama, who at the time was enjoying life in Geneva. Oyama had been out of the country during the Korean debate and was considered untainted by either side.

In October 1874, Oyama reluctantly left Switzerland and returned to Japan, heading at once for Kagoshima on Kyushu island. But Saigo was determined to have nothing more to do with politics, and his cousin returned to Tokyo, having failed in his mission. Later, in 1877, a group of antigovernment former samurai led by Saigo attacked the government forces at their Kumamoto camp, about 120 miles north of Kagoshima, in the so-called Satsuma Rebellion. Chosen to command the expeditionary force sent to put down the rebellion, Iwao Oyama stayed approximately six months in Kagoshima and Kumamoto. The fact that he had to fight against a cousin whom he most admired and respected left a scar on Oyama's soul that was to remain with him for the rest of his life.

In January 1876, Iwao Oyama married Sawako Yoshii, daughter of court advisor Tomomi Yoshii. The Yoshiis had the same Satsuma origins as Oyama, and it was Tomomi Yoshii who had traveled all the way to Paris to call his future son-in-law back to Japan to talk to Saigo. Sawako and Sutematsu were born the same year, so while Sutematsu was skating and bobsledding in New Haven with Alice and Marian Whitney, Sawako at the age of sixteen was already the wife of a major general.

Oyama doted on his young wife, who was still like a child in many ways. Although he had been forced to leave Europe before completing his studies, Oyama had high hopes that the government would send him there again, and in preparation he had Sawako study English. Her tutor was one Clara Whitney, a young woman not much different in age from her pupil. Clara's father, William (not to be confused with Yale professor of linguistics William Whitney), had been director of a business school in Newark when he was asked by Arinori Mori to set up a similar institution in Japan, and he had taken up the offer, bringing his family with him. In her book *Clara's Diary*, Clara often described Sawako as a pretty young woman and a fast learner.

In February 1880, Iwao Oyama was appointed minister of war. He was made a councilor in October of the following year. As one of the Chiefs of Staff he held an important position in the government, and any remaining hopes he had of being sent overseas to study again were effectively destroyed.

In the six years after their marriage Sawako gave birth to four girls, one of whom died. Tomeko, the youngest, born in 1882, was my father's mother. The first character of her name means "to stop," and according to my grandmother, it was often incorporated into the name of the youngest child as an expression of the mother's hope that there would be no more children.

Sawako never recovered from her last confinement, and after giving birth to Tomeko stayed in bed with a raging fever. It was a ferociously hot summer, and the young woman began to visibly slip away. To try and save his bedridden wife Oyama called in a German doctor, Erwin von Bäelze, but after taking one look at Sawako the doctor was forced to admit there was nothing he could do. Through his tears Oyama begged him to come every day anyway, just in case Sawako showed signs of recovery, and von Bäelze consented, out of sympathy for the distressed husband. As the doctor had predicted, however, there was no improvement, and on August 24, 1882, Sawako passed away. She was twenty-two. Von Bäelze had the following to say about her death:

> Today I witnessed the funeral of one of this country's outstanding women: the wife of General Oyama. She passed away two days ago, from puerperal fever, at the age of twenty-two. Mrs. Oyama was equally popular with foreign residents and her Japanese friends . . . so many times I had the pleasure of seeing her lovely face and hearing that mischievous laugh across the room at official functions. It seems but a short while since I last saw her well, on the emperor's birthday, and yet only a week ago when I was summoned to her side she was pale and drawn, and no longer conscious. It was already the third week of her illness when I was called, by which time it was too late to do anything. The general wanted me to see her every day, however, so I obeyed his wish and watched over her as she gradually slid toward death. The episode was a painful reminder of the helplessness of the medical profession in the face of certain illnesses, and of the incompetence of we human beings in general.
>
> (*Bäelze no nikki* [*Diary of Bäelze*], ed. by Toku Bäelze)

Having lost his beloved wife, Oyama constantly worried about his three daughters, who naturally were suffering from the loss of their mother. Fortunately Oyama's sister Kuniko had come up to Tokyo from Kagoshima and was looking after the girls. Women in Kagoshima were used to performing a variety of tasks from a young age—not just the obvious ones such as cooking and cleaning, but also the weaving of kimonos from silkworms they had raised themselves, and the planting and fermentation of soybeans to make miso (fermented soybean paste) and soy sauce—so there was no question of Kuniko not being able to look after the girls. But Oyama had been overseas, and he wanted his daughters to learn more than household chores: they needed a proper education. There was therefore no way that Kuniko, brought up in a region known even within Japan to be conservative and backward, and sporting a broad provincial accent, could be expected to educate the Oyama girls in the manner their father desired.

The solution seemed to be to find a suitable wife in the not too-far future—after the pain of Sawako's death had subsided—to whom Oyama could entrust his daughters' education. Sawako's father Tomomi Yoshii naturally wanted the best for his beloved grandchildren, and although the period of mourning for his daughter was not over, he used every means at his disposal to find his son-in-law a wife.

THE FIRST ENCOUNTER

There are many versions of how Iwao Oyama became acquainted with Sutematsu. One is that Oyama was in the audience when Sutematsu played Portia in *The Merchant of Venice*, and fell for her beauty and intelligence there and then. A biography of Takashi Masuda (Shigeko's brother) describes their meeting as follows:

> It was Shigeko Uryu who recommended Sutematsu to General Oyama. Shigeko had gone to America in 1871 as part of a group of five female students, of whom Miss Yamakawa was one, and she put a great deal of effort into ensuring that her friend became Mrs. Oyama. A meeting was arranged between the pair at the home of Shigeko's brother Takashi Masuda toward the end of 1883, and it was attended by Tsugumichi Saigo, Eiichi Shibuzawa, Nobushige Hozumi, Kaoru Inoue, the Uryus and the Masuda family. When everyone had gathered, several of those present put on a performance from *The Merchant of Venice* with Sutematsu as Portia, Sotokichi as Antonio, and Takashi's brother Eisaku as Shylock. The general sat

spellbound, never taking his eyes off Sutematsu as she delivered her lines in perfect English. It was a most unusual marriage meeting for the time.

As explained earlier, *The Merchant of Venice* was performed for Shigeko and Sotokichi's wedding reception: it was not planned to enable Oyama to meet Sutematsu. Moreover, the performance was in January 1883, not at the end of the year, so we can assume that the author's memory is faulty here, and that perhaps, in addition, his imagination has run away with him a little. That Oyama saw Sutematsu play Portia at the reception, however, is indisputable.

Oddly enough, it was Oyama's father-in-law Tomomi who actually suggested Sutematsu to the general. Iwao Oyama was known to be familiar with the latest Western fashions, having lived overseas for some time, and he also had many foreign friends. Then there was the question of the education of his three young daughters. The role of Oyama's wife could not be filled by an ordinary Japanese woman, and with that in mind Yoshii's attention was drawn to Sutematsu, who was blessed with both beauty and intelligence and had recently returned from America. Oyama had also seen Sutematsu at various functions, but Sawako had passed away less than a year before, so he was probably not thinking of Miss Yamakawa in terms of marriage. Yet, Yoshii's persistently glowing reports of the young woman, as well as what he had seen with his own eyes, convinced him that there could be no woman more suitable as his wife than Sutematsu. She was a slim beauty, the type he liked; her English was excellent, not to mention her ability in French and German, and she was the only Japanese woman to have graduated from college. The day was coming when Japan would be dealing with other nations on an equal basis, and Oyama knew that Sutematsu would cope with foreign visitors with ease, as well as be the ideal person to educate his daughters.

Yoshii passed on Oyama's request for Sutematsu's hand in marriage to the Yamakawas, who were floored by the proposal. How could they accept a military man of Satsuma origins as their daughter's husband? The Satsuma domain had betrayed the Aizu and left them branded as enemies of the throne, forcing them into exile in Tonami. No matter how many years passed, Aizu resentment toward Satsuma would not die after what the Aizu had suffered. Oyama was a superior of Sutematsu's brother Hiroshi, but even so there was no question of accepting the offer, and the family turned it down at once.

It was Tsugumichi Saigo, minister of agriculture and commerce and younger brother of Takamori Saigo, who said, "Leave this to me," and set out to convince the Yamakawas to accept his cousin Iwao's proposal. He visited the Yamakawa household several times, telling the family, "Now is the time to forget old feuds and join together: you must set an example for ordinary citizens and show your willingness to bury the past and work with each other to build a new Japan." Tsugumichi's persuasive argument had the desired effect, and the Yamakawas softened their attitude toward the proposal. They would accept it, but only if Sutematsu agreed.

When Sutematsu replied that she would give an answer only after she knew her prospective marriage partner better, the pair began to date. In an age when the individual rarely had any say in the choice of a marriage partner, this arrangement was very unusual indeed, but it seemed perfectly natural to two people who had lived overseas. Only those who were directly involved knew anything about Oyama's proposal, so the pair was restricted in their choice of places for outings.

I am so busy for I have more engagements than I know how to fill. One reason is that the distances are so great and I can not make more than one or two calls in one afternoon. The day before yesterday, I was invited to "lunch" by Mrs. Saigo who is the wife of the Minister of Agriculture. There were about twelve guests and everything done in the foreign style. The place was around five or six miles from here in the country where General Saigo has his summer home and General Oyama, Minister of War, asked us to go in his carriage so we did not have a very tiresome ride in the Jinrikishas. Then not long ago, General Oyama gave a dinner party and we were invited, so we had to go. I refuse all the invitations I possibly could [*sic*] but when I am invited by the Japanese I generally go for as a rule Japanese ladies are so retiring that they never go to parties and consequently when the ladies are not present men are not so careful of their behavior as they might be. I think the women should learn to mingle with men more and use their influence so that men won't go for singing girls and such for their amusement.

Of course the younger men who have been abroad are not so bad, but the older generation is just as bad as they can be. . . .

(April 12, 1883)

Sutematsu and Oyama had seen each other only a few times when she decided that he was the husband for her. Umeko, who had along with Sutematsu relished the prospect of being of service to Japan, could not contain her excitement over—and disappointment in—her longtime companion's pending marriage, and wrote to her host-mother, Mrs. Lanman:

And now I have reached the climax of my letter and the secret burning on the end of my pen is about to be put down. The secret in no longer a profound secret and Sutematsu says I may tell you. . . . Do you know our dear Sutematsu in a little while is going to be great lady, one of the first in the land in position as she is now in mind? In a few months, perhaps prolonged to six, Sutematsu has promised to marry Mr. Oyama, the Minister of War Department, and one of the Imperial cabinet, besides a great General. Are you not surprised? Is it not sudden? Sudden things seem to happen in Japan. Mr. Oyama is a great man, even higher than Mr.

Yoshida, because Mr. Yoshida is now only a vice-minister. I am very anxious to hear what you will say on this subject, your opinion on it. Need I say that this is a regular Japanese marriage? But Sutematsu was allowed freedom in her choice, and she decided for herself, though she grew thin with worrying and pondering and wavering, because it took much thought and foresight and resolution to do as she has, because it is for a lifetime. . . . I have been wild to tell you, but did not want to until Steam gave me permission. They had only seen each other a short while when Sutematsu decided, but not without much thought, I can tell you, and how Shige and she and I discussed it. Of course, I can't help being sorry that the marriage is not for love, but she could hardly have made a love match in Japan. Men don't see enough of the women to fall in love, and it is a rare case to marry for love anyhow, and she respects and likes him, and so that is right. *Then Sutematsu will not teach, of course; for the government, a sangi's* [councilor's] *wife teaching would be absurd* [emphasis added], and I am sorry to lose her help when I teach, for I must teach all alone. Then again Sutematsu will go out of our sphere and rank, be above us, and though she will never look down on us, yet I can't see as much of her as I do of Shige now after marriage. And she will be rather isolated as a great lady. But she can do wonderful good as a sangi's wife, when all the other great men's wives are former geishas, and she can help Japan.

(March 27, 1883)

Umeko understood, as Sutematsu did, that there was little freedom for women in Japan. Still, she was critical of Sutematsu's decision, although made of her own free will, to marry a man for reasons short of love. Umeko herself was to proclaim adamantly that she would never marry under pressure or to please anyone, and only for love if at all. She was to remain true to her words, and remained single throughout her life.

Three months after Sutematsu's decision to marry and the engagement were made public, she finally took her pen to write to Alice. It would be one of the most difficult letters she would ever have to write:

> Mr. Oyama was very urgent about making our engagement public, and so after considering the matter very carefully for two weeks, I have consented and we are formally engaged. Of course according to the Japanese custom, the usual ceremony of engagement took place and now we are bound to keep to our promises as if we were married. I would never take such a step without due consideration and I think I have done right. He is so thoroughly good that I am sure I may trust my future to him. I suppose you will not like it and I have thought over that too, but I felt that in questions of this nature one can not hope to please everybody. I felt somehow that I was ungrateful to you, but I know that you are too generous to think so. Besides, you would not wish that this feeling should prevent me from doing what I think would be for my future happiness and welfare. . . .
>
> Ume is busy too but not as happy as we would wish. She is misunderstood at home and feels all together very lonely and blue. You know we all feel that more or less but now I have something to look forward to and the feeling that one is necessary to someone's comfort and happiness is a wonderful cure for the worst blues and cheers me up to any kind of exertion. Although they all love me at home, I am not absolutely needed at home and the feeling that if I were dead, people would miss me but not mourn for me for very long used to make me very blue indeed. Mother has a grandson to whom she is wholly devoted, besides having lots other children beside myself. All my brothers and sisters are either married or have children. Shige has her husband, and so none of these people can be said to be dependent on me for their

comfort, but now it is different. I have someone whose happiness is in my keeping and whose children's welfare is in my hands. I do not mind all the small trials now come to me, for I don't pay them any attention but you have minded what it is to be wholly misunderstood sometimes. Japanese ideas and foreign ideas do not some times mingle well on some subjects and it is not an easy thing for the Japanese to look at the subject from any other point of view than their own. I hope to devote myself to my future husband's interests and try in every sense to be his helpmate. I feel that it is a very serious thing and I hope with God's help I shall be able to do my duty. . . . It all seems so strange and bewildering that I can't believe my senses. The idea of my getting married seems utterly impossible that some times I feel as if I were dreaming. I who used to say that marriage was not for such as I should actually promise to marry in three months seems rather unreal and unnatural.

My writing teacher has come so good bye. I hope you are not angry with me. It is for the best. My love to all. You can tell them of my engagement if you like for it is no secret now.

(July 2, 1883)

Not only was it no secret, the engagement seems to have garnered attention and curiosity. A foreigner commented:

I happened to be present when a bevy of young matrons fell upon Miss Yamakawa with congratulations and a host of questions. When would the marriage take place?—would it be a foreign wedding or a Japanese one?—was it a marriage of inclination or a marriage forced upon her? One silly young woman who wanted to show off exclaimed, "Stematsu [sic], how did you ever make up your mind to marry a man marked with smallpox?" "My dear," calmly responded Miss Yamakawa, "if you knew Count Oyama, you would never

think of his looks;" and true enough her words proved.
(*The Twentieth Century Home*, 1904)

A year earlier, Sutematsu had left New Haven dreaming of
working for her country, confident of being able to raise the level
of women's education in Japan to that of Europe and America
with the help of people such as Alice, whom she had intended to
bring to Japan as soon as possible. Viewed from America, it had all
seemed possible. But after twelve years away from Japan, even
Sutematsu herself did not realize the extent to which she had
become Americanized in her thinking; it was a shock on her
return to hit the centuries-old barriers of Japanese society.

As is obvious throughout the preceding letter, Sutematsu was
distressed that Alice would criticize her change of heart and accuse
her of betraying their mutual dream. Still, she also knew that no
matter how often she wrote, Alice was not in Japan and could
never be expected to understand the situation fully.

After her engagement to Oyama was officially announced in
June 1883, Sutematsu's days became even busier. Her thrice-week-
ly Japanese lessons continued, and in addition she began to receive
instruction in calligraphy twice a week. As the wife of a high government official she would be expected to be well dressed, and
thus had to put together a wardrobe. That chore was time-con-
suming, as each garment had to be specially fitted. And then, due
partly to Oyama's tastes, it was necessary to buy Western-style furniture for their new home, in addition to the traditional Japanese
bridal furnishings. Sutematsu was soon tired of all the formalities of
preparing for a Japanese wedding and grumbled to Alice, observing
the process as if she were a foreigner:

> The ceremony of formal engagement is very funny. He sends
> me all sorts of things and I have to send him same kind of
> things. The main thing in ordinary ceremony is the obie or
> the sash that women wear, which you know is the most

important and expensive feature of a lady's dressing: but in
my case as I don't intend to wear Japanese garments he sent
me white silk which he wishes to have made for the wedding
dress. It is heavy white silk and enough to make a long dress.
Besides the Japanese custom he followed the foreign fashion
and gave me a ring which looks all together too magnificent
on my scraggy fingers. . . .

As to our wedding preparations, we are in a considerable
perplexity, for we do not know whether we are to have the
regular Japanese or the foreign style. As to my outfit my family are much troubled for it has to be partly Japanese and partly
foreign. The regular Japanese trousseau consists of besides the
dresses and that sort of things [sic], bureaus, looking glasses,
wash basin, mousquitto [sic] netting, bed clothes, etc., etc. It
seems very absurd to take such things but the Japanese custom
is that you have to take them even if you have no dress but
the wedding dress.

(July 2, 1882)

Oyama had hoped to marry Sutematsu as soon as possible after
the first anniversary of Sawako's death (until which time it would
be considered too hasty), but the death of Tomomi Iwakura on
July 20 followed by those of the third and fourth daughters of the
Emperor Meiji in September meant that all festive events had to be
postponed until autumn as a sign of mourning.

On October 24, Oyama submitted his request for formal permission to marry to Grand Minister of State Sanetomi Sanjo (any
member of the cabinet who wished to marry required formal permission), and the following day reported his intentions in person to
the emperor. Five days later permission was granted, and the couple invited family and friends to the Japanese-style wedding set for
November 8. Oyama sent invitation cards written in French. On
November 8, 1883, Sutematsu became Mrs. Iwao Oyama, wife of
a councilor, lieutenant general, and minister of war. Exactly a year

had passed since she had returned to Japan, determined to spend her life in the service of women's education.

The Flower of
the Rokumeikan

THE OPENING OF
THE ROKUMEIKAN PAVILION

Approximately a month after the wedding, the couple were hosts of a reception at the newly renovated Rokumeikan guest house in Tokyo. Sutematsu was the perfect hostess, coping with the thousand guests at the Western-style event with seemingly effortless grace, and in a single evening she earned herself a place among the leading lights of high society. American reporter John Dwight described the occasion as follows:

The wedding was Japanese and no foreigners were invited, but directly afterward, on the 12th of December, 1883, Minister of War and Countess Oyama gave a ball to celebrate the event.

It would be difficult to imagine a more trying position than that of the young countess. Stepping from the threshold of college life into the position of a wife of the minister of war, she had had no training either for official life or for Japanese court etiquette, a thing so difficult and complicated that it takes years of practice to become an adept in its mysteries; yet this countess proved above the criticism of the most exacting observer.

About one thousand guests assembled that night—eight hundred Japanese and two hundred foreigners of all nationalities. Not only did the countess shake hands with each one upon arrival and again upon departure, but she made six bows to every Japanese present—a gymnastic feat which would have killed any American woman. Of course, it was not really four thousand eight hundred bows, for husband, wife and daughters arriving together would bow in union, so that three salutations would sometimes suffice to bid four guests welcome.

At that time, European customs were not fully understood by the Japanese, still another difficulty for the young hostess. When supper was served she left the ballroom and on the arm of Prince Komatsu led the way to the supper-room, followed by the corps diplomatique and the majority of her guests. Then, after they were seated and supper had begun, she was obliged to excuse herself to the prince and slip back to the ballroom to attend to the Japanese ladies, whose lords and masters, not being cognizant of foreign ways, had calmly left them to shift for themselves.

"A perfect hostess and the most delightful ball ever given in Tokyo," was the verdict.

(*The Twentieth Century Home*, 1904)

On November 28, three weeks after the Oyamas were married, the Rokumeikan pavilion had been officially opened with a gala event. Located near the imperial palace in Tokyo, on the site of the former Satsuma domain's residence, the Rokumeikan was a two-story brick building designed in an eclectic mixture of Greek, Spanish, and Islamic styles by a young government-employed British architect, Josiah Condor. Taking two years to complete at the exorbitant cost of 180,000 yen, the Rokumeikan contained a large dining room, lounges, meeting rooms, billiard room, and library on the first floor, and on the second a beautifully decorated ballroom and several guest rooms in which foreign visitors could stay.

It had long been a dream of the Meiji government to build an official guest house for foreign VIP visitors and residents and thereby impress upon the Western powers that Japan was modern and civilized. The Meiji government naively believed that if Japan appeared Westernized, the ongoing negotiations to revise the unequal treaties would go smoothly. The name "Rokumeikan," literally translated as "Deer Cry Pavilion," was derived from a Chinese poem in which a deer summons its companions by calling them, and alluded to the inviting call by Japanese leaders to the foreign community. Although "Rokumeikan" was the name of the guest house, it was also a symbol of the period when the Meiji government forced its people to imitate Western manners and customs.

It was Foreign Minister Kaoru Inoue who strongly pushed his idea of building a guest house to the government. After returning from two years' study in London in 1878, he recognized the urgent need for a facility for entertaining and accommodating foreign visitors in Tokyo. About that time, a number of distinguished people had traveled to Japan, including former United States President Grant, but the facilities in which they had been housed were far from adequate. In addition, Inoue was quite embarrassed to observe the government officials' ignorance of Western manners. He worried that high-ranking officials who drank the water from their finger bowls and fumbled with knives and forks would not help the country to be treated as an equal by its overseas treaty partners.

Once the Rokumeikan was complete, government officials, rich merchants, and the nobility—dressed in formal Western attire—flocked to it almost every night and entertained foreign guests with lavish dinners, concerts, and dancing. Despite the fact that some sarcastic Westerners likened them to monkeys when they wore suits, Japanese men who had never danced in their lives decked themselves out in tight tails and took gravely to the dance floor. For the first time wives also participated in social functions with their husbands, who might otherwise have brought geisha with them. The Rokumeikan was the only place where the women were on equal terms with their menfolk. Discarding their traditional kimonos, the ladies donned fashionable tight-fitting bustles, which emphasized the bustline and waist, and held hands with men in public for the first time as they waltzed under the glittering chandeliers. Bodies bound in restricting corsets, their feet unaccustomed to high heels, the society ladies of Tokyo bore it all in stoic determination to do their bit for the new Japan.

Foreign Minister Inoue and his wife were the hosts at the grand opening, to which approximately twelve hundred people had been invited. Those invited were naturally expected to bring their wives along, in accordance with Western tradition. Undoubtedly, the happiest man that evening was Iwao Oyama, who only three weeks earlier had married a beautiful and talented woman whose overseas experience was a perfect preparation for the dawning "Rokumeikan Era." With her shapely figure, fluent English, and charming manners, Sutematsu was soon the object of the other guests' admiration and was swiftly christened "the flower of the Rokumeikan." My grandmother once recalled, "Mother always looked beautiful in her evening dress." The outfit that had made such an impression on the young Tomeko eighty years earlier was a burgundy velvet dress ordered by Iwao Oyama and specially made in France. In her hair, Sutematsu wore three star-shaped diamond pins which glittered in the light so brilliantly that little Tomeko thought they were real stars from the sky. After the death of my grandmother, my great-aunt Takeko showed me a photograph of Sutematsu from the Rokumeikan days, and sure enough she was wearing the evening dress that Tomeko had described.

This first function at the Rokumeikan was followed rapidly by many more, and almost every night the building seemed to be filled with gorgeously decked-out ladies and gentlemen attending dinner parties and balls. Sutematsu's beauty and gracious bearing ensured that she was the belle of every ball. But even while she was twirling gaily around the polished wooden floors of the Rokumeikan, Sutematsu never forgot that she had once been a student whose education was paid for by the Japanese people. If by acting as hostess to foreign guests she could help Japan to Western-ize, and if by attending functions at the Rokumeikan and setting an example for other ladies of her class she could contribute to the improvement of their status as independent individuals, then she would gladly attend those functions every night. Sutematsu viewed this as one way of repaying her compatriots for the eleven years she herself had been fortunate enough to spend overseas.

In February 1884, still enjoying the happy afterglow of their marriage, the newlyweds were forced to separate for a year. Iwao Oyama was to be sent on his first official trip to Europe as minister of war. His mission was to observe the German military system and use the knowledge he gained to reform the existing one in Japan. The Meiji government had decided that the country should model its constitution and military on those of a constitutional monarchy such as Germany, where the Prussian king possessed the ultimate sovereign authority, much as the Japanese emperor did, rather than on a republic like France. The mission was a challenge to Oyama, who had spent much of his time in France, not Germany, and pro-fessed to be an expert on the French military.

Having seen her husband off, Sutematsu wrote to Alice for the first time in several months.

You must have given me up as a bad job when days and weeks passed away without a word from me. I have two very good reasons to offer you in excuse. One is that I have been quite sick—really sick you know so that I was obliged to stay in bed for two weeks. The second reason is that my husband was ordered to go to Europe and we were so busy with his preparations and entertainments given in consequence that until the day of his departure I had no time at all. He will be gone about a year and he thinks he may come home by way of America. He goes to Europe to inspect the armies of various countries and to introduce the best of their ways into ours. Just think, Alice, I might have gone too. Privately I was asked to go to Europe to study the ways and manners of the European courts and introduce the European ways into Japan and to reform our court. If I had consented I would have been officially asked by the court to make this tour. But I did not consent though our court needs reform more than anything else. If I told you all I know about the life of our Empress, you would think Japan was absolutely a barbarous country. The court is a separate world and the people [who] live in it do not know any other or care to know any better one. Some years ago it was much better and the Empress even went out on horseback with a side saddle, but now the reaction has set in so that it is worse than ten years ago. There are some prominent men who are very anxious to reform the court and to make it the leader of Western education and civilization.

(March 8, 1884)

Had not working with her husband for the good of the country been Sutematsu's most cherished wish? So when that wish was granted, why did she stay at home rather than accompany him to Europe? In her letter to Alice she was unusually reticent about her reasons for turning down the offer.

Sutematsu was in fact pregnant with the couple's first child; the illness she wrote of was most likely morning sickness. Sutematsu, aware of her condition, knew it would be unwise to embark on a thirty-day ocean voyage. She also knew that a pregnant wife would restrict her husband's movements, and the last thing she wanted to do was interfere with Oyama's ability to carry out an important state mission. To give birth to the child of someone she loves is naturally an occasion of great joy for a woman; nevertheless, Sutematsu strongly regretted not being able to travel with her husband.

Pregnancy was not the only thing stopping her from traveling to Europe: even if she were not with child, it was inconceivable that she should leave Oyama's three daughters—now her children too—for a year. The oldest, Nobuko, already eight years old, was a gentle and intelligent child, and she soon grew close to her new mother. The middle girl, Fuyuko, however, had been heavily influenced by the servants, who believed a stepmother to be inherently evil; she disobeyed Sutematsu at every turn, causing her a great deal of exasperation. Tomeko, the youngest, was still a baby, and unable to differentiate Sutematsu from her real mother. One day on the way home from primary school, however, a friend told her, "That mother you've got now isn't really your mother, you know," then continued, "This is your mother," and covered one eye, the sign for "mistress." The shocked Tomeko ran home and told Sutematsu, who replied that what her friend said was nonsense, of course she was mommie's little girl. But Tomeko had already sensed something was not quite right. Now she knew for certain that Sutematsu wasn't her mother and understood why, every year on August 24, Sutematsu would take out a picture of a strange woman and place it on the piano, then decorate it with flowers and make the girls put their hands together in prayer. When little Tomeko would ask who the lady was, Sutematsu would reply, "A lady who is always looking down from heaven making sure you're being a good girl." That day was the anniversary of Sawako's death.

In a letter to Alice four months after her wedding, it was evident that Sutematsu had whole-heartedly taken on the role of mother for her three Oyama daughters.

> Although you might think I had a great deal of time now since my husband went away, but I have much to do. Besides the ordinary duties of housekeeping, I teach six small children almost every afternoon. They are the children of some friends of my husband's and my oldest little girl. It is a hard work teaching English to children for they will not study at home or prepare their lessons.
>
> I have had a dreadful time with the children. First one got a mild form of pleurisy which was followed by malarial fever. Just as that one got over her turn, another got scarlatina, which is epidemic, so that two of my servants got sick, but you may imagine my feeling when the little one got so feverish and red. She is all right now.
>
> (April 20, 1884)

A NEW SCHOOL FOR
THE FEMALE ARISTOCRACY

Sutematsu's pregnancy prevented her from traveling to Europe with her husband, but not from tackling a major assignment while he was away. An opportunity to aid in the setting up of a new school for the daughters of families of the aristocracy unexpectedly came her way.

At the time, children of the imperial and aristocratic families were educated at the Peers School in Kanda, on the same site as the University of Tokyo. In 1877 there were two hundred boys at the school and a mere fifty-nine girls, but as the upper class became more interested in educating its daughters, the roll increased until the school buildings could no longer accommodate the flood of new students. The result was a plan to build a new girls' school administered directly by the Imperial Household

Department, on land in Yotsuya belonging to the emperor, and Sutematsu was chosen by Minister Hirobumi Ito of the department to assist in setting it up.

Sutematsu had been dismayed by the feudalistic trappings of the imperial court on her occasional visits, and felt strongly that any headway in women's higher education might well be achieved through reform of Japan's aristocracy. Ecstatic that she would finally be able to use some of her talents, she wrote Alice:

> I have been so busy that I had no time to finish this letter. Do you know that the dream of my life is to be now realized? As I wrote the other day that our court is in very much need of reform but that it was next to an impossibility to improve it by any direct means, some prominent men who have a great deal of influence have thought of a school under the patronage of the Empress. You know there are [sic] no school for girls which may be considered in any way decent. In fact there are only two schools beside the primary schools, which are for girls, and both of which [are] perfectly wretched. Of course there are missionary schools, but they too are defective in many ways: besides the higher classes will not let their daughters attend such schools. So you see Japan is sadly in need of a thoroughly good girls school—not college, for girls education will not go as high as that—and also the court needs reform. The latter object is to be obtained by means of the former, so kill two birds with one stone. As the school is to be partly supported by the court, the Empress and the ladies of the court will be obliged to visit the school, by which means education and western ideas are to introduced [sic] to the very center of court.
>
> Of the committee of two to establish this school, I have been asked to be one. We are to set up a school just as we think best with no one to interfere, with much money to command, with the support of the most influential men of

Japan. Is not that just what I should like? The other lady has now a school of her own which she established two years ago. She is a woman of a great deal of character and experience besides being a deep thinker. She has been one of the maids of honor and was a great favorite with the Empress. At first I declined the offer for this position but I was urged so strongly, I was obliged to yield. Mr. Ito whose idea it is to establish this school, was so strong in his arguments that I could not say anything. He brought forth three reasons: one that I had moral obligation toward Japan for I was sent to America by its government. The next that I was the only woman in Japan who had received a degree from a college. The third that I was placed in a very prominent and influential position, being the wife of a cabinet minister.

(March 8, 1884)

The other woman mentioned in Sutematsu's letter is Utako Shimoda. Utako had been employed as a lady-in-waiting for seven years before her marriage, and was regarded with great affection by the empress for her erudition and abilities in Japanese poetry. Despite having a sick husband to care for, she was an active supporter of women's education, and in 1882 had opened a private girls' school in her home, for daughters of high-ranking officials. Two years later, after her husband died, Utako returned to the court. Her school, called "Toyojojuku," was later absorbed into the Peeresses' School.

Hirobumi Ito described her as "an amazing woman: she possesses great knowledge and brilliant insight. She is extremely eloquent, and if she were a man I have no doubt she would be a minister by now." Blessed with beauty as well as brains, Utako Shimoda joined Sutematsu as one of the stars of high society.

The two talented women went to work—and Sutematsu put to use her knowledge of Vassar College and its course of studies. The Imperial Household Department spent a year deciding on lesson

content and school rules, at the conclusion of which the new Peeresses' School was opened in October 1885 with much support
from the empress. Enrollment was triple that of the old school.
Lieutenant General Kanjo Tani was appointed principal. Utako
Shimoda taught and was in charge of administration, but in actual
fact she did all the principal's paperwork as well. Sutematsu's position as wife of the minister of war, and thus, part of the aristocracy, made it unacceptable in society's view for her to teach; once
the school opened, she restricted further contributions to what
could be done out of the public eye.

Umeko Tsuda's name appeared on the school's staff list on the
opening day. Lonely and depressed, Umeko had met Hirobumi Ito
accidentally at the grand ball for the emperor's birthday approximately a year after her return from the United States. Their last
meeting had been ten years before that, in Washington. Hearing
about her unhappy circumstances, Ito felt sorry for the girl and
offered her a live-in job as English tutor to his wife and daughter,
and arranged for her to teach English at Utako Shimoda's school.
With the opening of the new Peeresses' School, Umeko shifted
there to teach.

Like Sutematsu, Umeko also felt let down by Japanese society
on her return from America. Unlike Sutematsu and Shigeko, she
unfortunately had no supportive home environment. Although
Sutematsu was instrumental in getting a teaching position for
Umeko, her reservations about Umeko's future are clear:

> I feel so sorry for Ume because she does not find the lan-
> guage easy to learn besides her home is not so happy as mine.
> Her family are all Christians but they, at least her father, is
> [*sic*] very queer and Ume does not find her home happy. . . .
> Ume is really quite unhappy especially when she had so much
> petting in America, and made much of. Ume's father or any
> of them do not understand her at all and she feels that she has
> no sympathy from them at all. . . . I don't see what can be

done for poor Ume unless we get her married. She is not suited to teach: even if she were she won't be able to for a year or two and if we leave her long at her home I am sure her father will marry her off to some body who will not make her happy.

(January 18, 1883)

THE CHARITY BAZAAR

Very few people knew of Sutematsu's assistance in founding the Peeresses' school, but the same cannot be said for the leading part she played in organizing Japan's first charity bazaar, at a time when hardly anyone in the country had even heard of the word "charity."

I have not yet told you that I have started a fair in aid of our new poor-hospital. Such a thing has never been done in Tokio and so this is the first of its kind. The Japanese, I am sorry to say, have not much idea of work of charity, but they have all taken very kindly to the idea. The whole Tokio is to come to it, but it is to be by ladies only and these only of the higher classes. About 150 ladies have promised to contribute to the fair and it will be quite a large thing. You don't how [sic] such a thing strikes the Japanese for hitherto nobody ever thought of public charity. But I hope it will succeed not only account [sic] of the hospital but also for the general good of the Japanese, for this will teach them how necessary it is to give charity. We hope to realize at least a thousand yen. So you see I am busy there too, for the Japanese need rousing up so that I have to go about a great deal. Of the committee of six for the fair, one is Mrs. Ito (Mr. Ito is our Minister of the Imperial Household and it is his family where Ume stays as a sort of governess and companion), my sister (who went to Russia) who is now one of the maids of honor to the

Empress; Ume is one besides two others and myself. I must close for I must write to others.

Good-bye. Write to me for it is an age since I heard from you.

(April 20, 1884)

Sutematsu on one occasion had been given the opportunity to inspect the Yushi Kyoritsu Tokyo Hospital (the present-day Jikei University School of Medicine), and that visit had prompted the idea of the bazaar. Having attended nursing school in New Haven only two years previously, she was interested in seeing how Japanese nurses compared with their American counterparts. To her surprise, the patients were being attended by male nurses. There and then she questioned the hospital's director:

"You must know that women do this kind of work overseas, so why don't you use them here?" she asked, adding that females were naturally more patient and caring and therefore more suited to nursing. The director replied that he agreed entirely, but that the hospital simply did not have the funds to build a nursing school.

At that point, Sutematsu recalled her experiences with "Our Society" in New Haven and determined to organize a bazaar in Tokyo to raise funds for a nursing school. Today the words "bazaar" and "charity organization" are part of everyday vocabulary in Japan, but a hundred years ago the idea of working to raise money for complete strangers or organizations was unheard of. The upper class particularly regarded money with distaste—as something soiled and handled only by merchants. To have the wives and daughters of the nobility opening stalls and actually selling things shocked polite society. It was a revolutionary concept.

For three days beginning on June 12, 1884, the Rokumeikan, never out of the limelight since its opening, was once again the center of attention as Sutematsu and her aristocratic ladies held their "Rokumeikan Charity Bazaar." The event received wide coverage in the papers even before it began, and over the three days during which the bazaar was held, officials and members of the imperial families arrived in droves by carriage and jinrikisha to see what all the fuss was about.

The second floor of the building was crammed with stalls displaying the handiwork of Sutematsu's ladies. Tempting the curious hordes were dolls, *tabi* (socks), handkerchiefs, neckpieces for kimonos, hats, bamboo ware, and confectionery, all at prices far above normal. Anyone who thought he was just there for a look soon realized his mistake: the waiting women had no intention of letting window-shoppers pass them by. Naturally few were brave enough to resist the sales pitch of the wife of a high-ranking government official, and most gave in and made a purchase. Hapless shoppers paying for a four-yen purchase with a five-yen note were told that change was not given at a bazaar, and had little choice but to silently curse their ignorance and pay up.

Japan's first charity bazaar was a financial success, attracting twelve thousand people over the three days it was open and earning an incredible eight thousand yen—several times Sutematsu's most optimistic estimate. As promised, all the proceeds were donated to the Yushi Kyoritsu Tokyo Hospital.

Sutematsu continued to take an interest in the training of nurses, and did her best to make it widely known that in Western countries they were highly valued and respected members of society. She urged the Japanese Red Cross to play a part in training them. As a result, the Red Cross Ladies Volunteer Nursing Association began operating in June 1887. Its founders were a group of women from the imperial families and nobility, chiefly Princess Arisugawanomiya. However, such women could not be expected to have any actual knowledge of nursing, and Sutematsu provided the driving force behind the association.

THE COSTUME PARTY

In January 1885, Iwao Oyama returned from his year-long tour of Europe and the United States. Sutematsu was already a mother by then, not of a boy as Oyama had hoped, but of another girl, who was named Hisako.

With her husband's return, Sutematsu's days became even busier than before, occupied by both public and private concerns, including care of the children and the management of the house. In Oyama's absence the government had rearranged the order and ranking of nobility after the European system. Oyama was now raised to the rank of a count by the Peerage Act of July 1884. At the end of the following year, Ito abolished the Supreme Council of State formed at the time of the Restoration and introduced a cabinet system after the German model. Ito became the first prime minister and Oyama was once again minister of war. Now with the title of Countess Oyama, wife of the minister of war, Sutematsu's position among the very highest ranking members of society was indisputable.

The years between 1885 and 1888 constituted the golden era of the Rokumeikan, with balls and receptions taking place almost every night. Both having lived overseas, Sutematsu and her husband were considered forerunners of the "Rokumeikan Era" and central figures on the social scene. A party held at their official residence on the evening of January 27, 1887, was considered the most successful yet, either in or out of the Rokumeikan, and Sutematsu's careful preparation and poised performance as hostess was as impressive as ever.

On April 20 of the same year, a fancy ball was held at the official residence of Prime Minister Ito, a symbolic event that was to become the most talked about of the Rokumeikan period. Imitating Western practices to facilitate treaty revision was one thing, but that ball went beyond a sense of duty and entered the realm of the ludicrous.

At half past nine, the host and his wife Count and Countess Ito, dressed as Italian nobles, greeted their distinguished guests many of whom—including the governor of Tokyo, several prominent businessmen, and Kaoru Inoue, the man who had worked so hard to bring the Rokumeikan into existence—appeared as figures from famous Japanese legends. Wearing a variety of costumes, some gorgeous, some comic, they took themselves too seriously to recognize how ridiculous they looked to those not participating. Iwao Oyama, as a Satsuma warrior, wore a samurai-style wig, hardly an adventurous choice for him, and Sutematsu, to match her husband, dressed as a traditional female merchant of Kyoto, making a rare excursion into the world of Japanese clothing. She carried firewood and wooden implements on her head.

The boisterous merrymaking at the ball, which lasted until three o'clock in the morning, caught the attention of nationalists—already none too pleased with the extreme Westernization policy of the government—as well as of others seriously concerned about the future of the country. The newspapers had a field day, attacking the government leaders for their superficial admiration of Western culture. One of their targets was an unwitting Sutematsu, as may be seen from this article in the May 5 edition of the *Choya Shinbun* paper:

> Since the marriage of Sutematsu, sister of Major General Yamakawa, to Minister of War Oyama, the couple have shown nothing but the greatest affection toward each other, drawing much envy from their acquaintances. Now it seems however that they are discussing divorce, and rumor has it that Mrs. Oyama will be returning to her family soon.

Sowing the seeds of suspicion while providing nothing in the way of facts, the article is little different from those written by gossip columnists today.

Sutematsu had given Oyama a long-awaited son in February of the previous year, and was in fact three months pregnant when the article appeared. Despite the difference in their ages, the pair had a loving and trusting relationship, and when Sutematsu called her husband by his first name in the American manner, a beaming smile would break out over his face.

Described as having "a heart as big as the ocean," Iwao Oyama was also known for his marvelous sense of humor, and true to his first name—which means "large boulder"—never let himself be pressured into action by people or circumstances, although he hated disputes. He was one of the few high-ranking government officials who had never shown an interest in having concubines or visiting geisha houses. If Sutematsu had asked for a divorce, as the article alleged, he probably would have granted her one, just as he would have granted any wish of the woman he loved. And Sutematsu, as she had shown in the Naibu Kanda episode, was a level-headed woman in most matters, so it is doubtful that she would have wanted to leave her husband on some passion-inspired impulse. The intention of the article clearly was to criticize the government-sponsored Westernization of Japanese women, symbolized by Sutematsu's role at the Rokumeikan.

Insulted and hurt by the article, Sutematsu stopped attending balls at the Rokumeikan and other high-profile functions of her class. She spent more time at home, focusing her energy on bringing up her brood of children. Umeko observed of her friend:

> She just stays in the house and minds children, and looks after things, and is a figure head, while all her studying and accomplishments go for nothing. . . . You see Japan is in such a whirl now, and the question of women's education etc., being so much agitated that any woman as Mrs. Shimoda or Sutematsu, who is in any way prominent or well known is picked to pieces. . . .

Drunk from wine and the heady excitement of novelty, Tokyo's upper class forgot its traditional values, and the Rokumeikan was the scene of behavior that outraged public opinion and added fuel to the growing fire of opposition to the government. With the resignation of Foreign Minister Kaoru Inoue, who had failed to obtain treaty revision after eight years of fighting, the glorious days of the Rokumeikan came to an abrupt end.

Sutematsu lost her third child at the end of 1887. The eldest daughter, Nobuko, had never regained her strength after a childhood bout with pleurisy, and that winter she caught a severe cold. Sutematsu, who was pregnant, was treating her with an inhaler when the device suddenly exploded, shocking Sutematsu into premature labor. The baby died two days after it was born. While the explosion was the direct cause of the tragedy, it is likely that the newspaper article, combined with a hectic round of functions, took its toll; the short-lived daughter, named Nagako, was in a way a tragic sacrifice to the "Rokumeikan Era." Two years later, in 1889, Sutematsu gave birth to her second son, Kashiwa, making a total of four pregnancies during the height of the Rokumeikan era. That means that Sutematsu was always carrying a child then, and we can only imagine the possible mental and physical tortures she endured as a participant in an endless succession of balls and receptions.

Turning Inward

ALICE BACON COMES TO JAPAN

At the beginning of 1888, wonderful news aroused Sutematsu from the depression she had suffered since the loss of her child and the newspaper stories. Alice was finally on her way to Japan.

Unfortunately, the letters that Sutematsu wrote Alice between 1886 and 1888 have been lost, so we do not know precisely under what circumstances Alice came to Japan. The records of the Peeresses' School, now the Joshi Gakushuin, which invited her, give no clues either. But it is easy enough to imagine how Sutematsu, as a member of the committee setting up the school, and Umeko, who was teaching in its English department, could have recommended Alice to the Imperial Household Department.

Sutematsu and Umeko pinned their hopes of realizing their cherished dream—using the ten years they had spent abroad to benefit women's education in Japan—on the new school. Yet on closer examination, they found that the qualities the school was nurturing in Japanese women were no different from those that had been considered desirable for centuries. School regulations exhorted "all those who learn here" to "be a good wife to your husband, a wise mother to your children, and look after your in-laws." The young women of the noble families were told to "culti-vate the virtues expected of a lady of your station, neither be taken by superficial appearances nor be carried away by imagination, and apply what you have learned to your life." Umeko found her work extremely frustrating, and her exasperation with the immaculately groomed, doll-like students who seemed to hold no opinions of their own grew with each passing day.

She and Sutematsu hoped that by putting Alice—a woman who had chosen to dedicate her life to education rather than to a home and family—in front of the girls, they could effect some small change in them.

Alice Bacon was a woman of great strength and determination. She had been interested in racial issues from an early age, under the strong influence of her father. At the age of twelve she determined to spend her life helping to improve black education, for even after emancipation ex-slaves were subject to crippling discrimination. When Sutematsu arrived at the Bacon home in New Haven, Alice was already spending her summers teaching at the Hampton Nor-mal and Agricultural Institute in Virginia, where her half-sister Rebecca was the assistant principal, and in 1883, the year Sutemat-su married, she became a full-time teacher. When Alice found out that several training schools for nurses had refused entry to one of her black students, she collected donations and built a hospital with its own nursing school right in Hampton.

Alice arrived in Tokyo in June 1888, accompanied by her faith-ful collie, Bruce. Unable to contain their excitement at seeing her for the first time in six years, Sutematsu, Shigeko, and Umeko renewed their vows of friendship and promises to work together for women's education.

Alice rented a house near the school with Umeko, and the two of them lived there with another teacher from the school, three pupils, and several servants. Thus Alice began her life in Japan almost completely surrounded by Japanese. Later, after her one-year contract expired and she returned to the United States, Alice wrote about her experiences in the book *A Japanese Interior*, published by Houghton, Mifflin and Co. in 1894.

Alice described her place of employment in detail. The girls whom Sutematsu and Umeko found irritating and unsatisfactory as students Alice saw as well-mannered and proud, but on her first day at the school, she quickly realized that her pupils had never had any freedom to express themselves as independent individuals.

> After a while it was announced that all the teachers and pupils were to assemble in the gymnasium, there to be addressed by the principal, an elderly and scholarly gentleman of the old school, but one who speaks not a word of English. We went down to the gymnasium, which is connected with the main school building by a covered walk, and met all the girls on their way thither, each class under the leadership of a teacher. . . . When we finally reached the gymnasium, we found it filled with girls arranged in line according to size, with all the smallest ones in front. When I saw them, my thoughts could not but fly back to Hampton, and contrast our poor little pickaninnies there with these little peeresses. But they are alike in one way, and that is that their lives are more or less stunted and cramped by the circumstances of their birth, the pickaninnies by poverty and the disabilities of their low social position, the peeresses by the rigid restraints and formalities that accompany their rank.
>
> Very pretty children these little peeresses are, in spite of the ugly foreign dress into which the school requirements force them. Their mothers have undoubtedly tried hard to have them well dressed for the first day of school, but most of the dresses have evidently been chosen and made by people

not in the least familiar with any style of European garment, and are now worn in such a way as to make the children look, so far as clothes go, like the veriest clodhoppers, instead of the descendants of perhaps the oldest aristocracy in the world. . . . But there the children stand in their queer clothes, all silent and orderly, though no one is keeping order, and the teachers are bustling about, talking among themselves. Any company of American children would be uncontrollable if kept standing so long with nothing to do, but these children are too well mannered to be noisy in the presence of their elders, and so they stand like statues and wait.

(September 17, 1888)

As a teacher at the Peeresses' School, Alice had the opportunity to mix with members of the imperial family and noble class. Naturally she was accepted by the Oyamas as one of the family, and when she visited, the oldest son, Takashi, would climb on to "Aunty Bacon'"s knees and refuse to budge.

Alice's one-year stay in Tokyo coincided with a number of significant events in Japanese history, and she describes them vividly in her book. The year 1889 was the last year of the Rokumeikan's functions, its glitter like the momentary brilliance of fireworks. Near the end of 1888, Alice was invited to a Rokumeikan ball held by the naval minister, Tsugumichi Saigo.

The past week has been quite a gay one in my quiet life. I do not know whether I told you that I had been invited to a ball given by one of the cabinet ministers. It was held at the Rokumei-kwan, or Nobles' Club. The building is in foreign style, and handsomely fitted up with foreign furniture. It was beautifully decorated for the occasion with plants, flowers, and flags, and the grounds were illuminated with lanterns. The ball was given for the foreign naval officers, and was not a very large one,—only four or five hundred invitations issued,—so the rooms were not at all crowded. At such an entertainment as this there is one drawing-room and a small dining-room set apart for the aristocracy,—princes, princesses, counts, countesses, etc. From this retreat the nobility come out and mingle with the crowd when they like, but the crowd is not expected to go in and mingle with the nobility to any great extent. . . . Led by my more daring escort, I ventured in thither, and there saw the princesses all sitting in a row, looking very uncomfortable in their stiff, foreign dresses, and quite bored beside. The princes were mostly outside dancing with the multitude, and when we returned to the ball-room my friends pointed them out. They did not seem to me very impressive in appearance, but have an exceedingly aristocratic way of holding up their heads that makes up somewhat for their small stature.

The thing that struck me most on going into the dancing-room was the amazing number of men in gorgeous uniforms and the very small sprinkling of ladies, mainly foreign, and all in foreign dress. There was an open space in the centre of the floor, in which the dancers enjoyed themselves, and around the edges was a solid phalanx of men, looking on at the evolutions of their brethren who had been fortunate enough to secure partners. Apropos of the small number of women, I heard rather a funny story from a lively little Japanese lady to whom I was introduced. She spoke English prettily, though with a strong accent, and was being instructed in the latest style in foreign clothes by an American friend when I came up. When I remarked to her on the small number of ladies present, she laughed heartily as she told me of a gentleman who had come to her that evening and asked her to find him a young lady as a partner. She said that she did not know any young lady whose card was not already full. "Well, then," was the reply, "find me an old lady, for I must dance." But no old lady could be found, so the would-be dancer was obliged to

join the ranks of the male wall-flowers who formed so notice-
able a feature of the affair.

(November 25, 1888)

About a month after New Year's, the new Japanese Imperial
Constitution was promulgated. Hirobumi Ito and other prominent
politicians and scholars had drafted it after spending two years
observing and studying Germany's constitutional monarchy. As the
new constitution provided for the diet system with a cabinet and
an independent judiciary, Japan could now point proudly to those
trappings of a modern state when negotiating with Western powers. In reality, however, sovereignty was held by the sacred and
unassailable emperor, the Diet was within his control, and the military was answerable only to the throne. The constitution's strong
military flavor reflected its writers' adherence to the slogan of the
times: "Wealthy country and strong army" (*fukoku kyohei*).

The new constitution was promulgated amid great fanfare on
the morning of February 11, 1889, at the newly built imperial
palace. A heavy snowfall from the previous evening blanketed the
area around the imperial residence in white. Lanterns and Japanese
flags lined the streets, and people were in a festive mood.

After attending the school's own celebration of the event, Alice
and her students stood outside the gate for two hours, watching
the grand procession.

> After these exercises were over, we put on our wraps, and
> went out and stood in line for an hour in front of the build-
> ing, and watched the funny Japanese crowd until the proces-
> sion came by. Upon this occasion, for the first time, the
> Emperor and Empress rode in the same coach, and it is really
> a great step up, so far as the women of the country are con-
> cerned. The theory hitherto has been that the Emperor is too
> far above his wife in dignity to appear in public with her in
> the same carriage, but yesterday, by riding with her, he rec-

ognized the fact that his wife is raised by her marriage to his own social level. It is a formal adoption of the Western idea in regard to the position of the wife.

The procession was the finest that I have seen yet. First there were the mounted, gold-laced soldiers, carrying red and white pennons, who always march in front of the Emperor's carriage. These were followed by four or five state coaches, containing the princes and cabinet ministers. Then came another squad of horsemen, and then the most gorgeous coach that I have ever seen, drawn by six black horses, each led by a magnificent black, white, and gold liveried groom, while the coachman on the box was so bedizened with gold that he looked like a lay figure rather than a real man. Just at this point we all bowed, so that I saw nothing more but the top of the Empress' bonnet as she turned to look at her little peeresses, who seem to have a warm place in her heart. When we lifted our heads, the splendid vision was gone, and there was nothing more to see except every-day black carriages, which seemed very tame after the state coaches. After the procession proper had passed, there came an indiscriminate medley of things that had been accumulating behind the detachment of police who had kept the road clear. The dam once removed, they swept down upon us like a flood: the populace in all degrees of mud and jollity; big-bugs with gold lace in kurumas [jinrikisha]; bigger bugs with more gold lace in carriages; horsemen, foot-soldiers, artillery,—all in one grand mêlée. Why nobody was walked on by the horses or run over by the gun-carriages I do not at all understand, but nobody was, at least in our neighborhood.

(February 12, 1889)

While Alice was watching the celebrations with her pupils, a man whom the Bacon family, Sutematsu, Shigeko, and Umeko had had a long association with was assassinated. Minister of Education Ari-

nori Mori, the man who with Kiyotaka Kuroda had proposed to
the new Meiji government the idea of sending females abroad to
study, and who thus was instrumental in changing the fate of three
little girls, was stabbed by a low-ranking official of the Ministry of
Interior. Alice remembered him as one of the few Japanese with
whom her father, Leonard Bacon, had been intimately associated.

But during these two days of festival a tragedy was also enact-
ed, and on the day on which Japan gained a Constitution she
lost one of her most enlightened and liberal-minded statesmen. I am going to write out all the details as I had them
directly from the lips of one of the cabinet ministers, for I
suppose many reports of the affair will reach America, and it
may be interpreted as a sign of a reactionary tendency and an
outbreak of mediævalism, and I do not think that it can really
be attributed to that. The facts, as they are at present known
to the authorities, are these, and I give them as I heard them,
on the morning of Viscount Mori's death.

On Monday, February 11, as Viscount Mori was dressing
to go to the palace for the promulgation ceremony, a man
came to the door of his official residence and asked to see the
viscount. . . . Just then Viscount Mori himself came down the
long hall, on his way to his carriage. As he passed, the secretary said to him, "This is the man who wanted to see you."
Mr. Mori stopped for a moment, the man stepped forward,
and before any of the bystanders could see what he was about,
he drew a long, sharp knife from his clothing with his left
hand, while with his right he seized Mr. Mori, and then, with
a quick movement, plunged the knife into the minister's right
side. He had not had time to pull out the knife and strike
again when the servants pulled him off, but he broke away
from them, and was at once cut down and killed by the sword
of a policeman who came in from his station at the gate, as he
heard the noise of the struggle. . . .

And now as to the reasons for the murder. A paper was found upon the body of the assassin, saying that the viscount had been killed because of sacrilege committed by him the year before at the shrines of Isé. It appears that the minister had visited these, the most sacred of Shinto shrines, and when there had failed to make the customary offerings, had refused to take off his boots before entering the sanctuary, and is said to have even pushed aside the curtain that concealed the sacred treasures. Many conservative Japanese of the lower classes were much worried by this, and were afraid that the protection of the national gods might be withdrawn from a government in which so godless a person was prominent; and the sacrilege so rankled in the heart of this man, who was a humble employee of the government, that he resolved to rid the country of its perpetrator, that the protection of the guardian spirits might not be withdrawn upon the change to a new form of government. . . . He undoubtedly committed the act from patriotic and religious motives, and not from a mere grudge, but he does not, so far as I can find out, represent any public sentiment, nor is any portion of the population pleased that his patriotism and religion should have taken such a form. It is a misfortune that he should have been killed on the spot instead of having to take his trial, for such summary justice often excites sympathy, when a legal trial and condemnation does not, and in a trial much could have been found out about the man which now will never be known.

(February 15, 1889)

Alice returned to America, taking memories of a turbulent period in Japanese history. It is doubtful whether during her short sojourn she was able to influence her doll-like students to any great extent, considering that they had been inculcated with such a different set of values, but her book *A Japanese Interior* became a valuable reference work for Americans in an age when very little was written in English about the everyday lives of the Japanese people.

While teaching at the Peeresses' School, Umeko had been having grave doubts about her work and lifestyle. She discussed with Alice her pet plan to return to America, this time to study a new teaching method that would further contribute to the improvement of women's education in Japan. Granted a two-year leave of absence with pay from the Peeresses' School, Umeko left for the United States a month earlier than Alice, to enroll in Bryn Mawr College near Philadelphia, Pennsylvania.

THE IMPERIAL VISITS

Meanwhile, looking after six children and supervising the Oyama legion of over twenty servants kept Sutematsu busy. Unlike most high-ranking government officials, her husband had no interest in the "teahouses" frequented by geisha, and turned down as many evening engagements as he could get away with in order to spend time with his wife and family. Oyama preferred Western food to Japanese, so before the family hired a new cook it was Sutematsu's job to test the applicant's omelette-making skills to ascertain whether that person was suitable for the post. My grandmother Tomeko, tiring of the constant diet of Western food, would occasionally sneak into the kitchen, where the servants would prepare her a simple treat of steaming white rice sprinkled with *katsuobushi* (dried bonito flakes) and soy sauce.

Apart from her duties as wife of a cabinet minister, Sutematsu held the post of "Advisor on Westernization in the Court." Asked in 1888 for assistance by the Imperial Household Department, she made frequent visits to the palace to advise the empress on Western manners and dress and to act as an interpreter for foreign visitors. As she confided to Alice in her letters, she hoped that contact with a woman like herself, who had lived overseas, would go some small way toward liberating the empress and her attendants from their old-fashioned ways of thinking.

In the winter of 1889, the Oyamas moved from the minister's

official residence to a new house. Built by a German architect, the structure had been finished in time for a visit from the emperor, who had taken to seeing his leading ministers in their homes—a first in Japanese history—in order to cultivate a closer relationship with them and their families.

The house was in Onden, present-day Harajuku, an area now filled with fashionable boutiques and busy fast-food shops. In those days, however, according to Tomeko, "you could hear foxes howling nearby." In that lonely spot a five-story red brick house, complete with weather vane on the roof, suddenly appeared. Oyama had bought the land of twenty-one thousand square meters for a thousand yen, and spent twenty thousand yen on the house itself. Ten years later Sutematsu's friend Marian Whitney visited her and described the house as follows:

> One long day we spent at her home, a large house in extensive grounds a little outside the city. General Oyama was fond of European ways. He was a large heavy man and hated sitting on the floor and as an officer he wore a uniform which made life à la Japanese almost impossible. The house was quite foreign, a large red brick building, very ugly, I grieve to say, in the style of the 80's and furnished in rather florid style with furniture bought by him in France, but there was a long, low Japanese wing in which the children lived for the most part, sleeping, sitting and eating on the floor in true Japanese style, for their mother was too wise to bring them up as strangers to the customs of their own country.
>
> (*Vassar Quarterly*, July 1919)

The emperor visited this new home in November 1890. A photograph taken to mark the grand and honored occasion shows the Oyama family lining up in front of a rather odd building, which appears to be a cross between a medieval European castle and the country home of a European noble. Oyama is in dress uniform,

Sutematsu in a dark dress, and the daughters in Japanese kimono. The children were brought up wearing Western clothing, and Tomeko recalled the excitement she felt on receiving her first kimono, bought especially for the visit of the emperor and empress.

Sutematsu had received the empress dowager and the empress two weeks earlier, so the two occasions back to back no doubt caused her much stress. The emperor's visit was a great success, however, with the emperor arriving at one in the afternoon and staying until ten in the evening—far beyond the scheduled time of the visit—enjoying the performances of Noh drama, music, and recitation of Chinese poetry staged for his benefit. As hostess, Sutematsu must have been more than satisfied with her guest's reluctance to leave.

Two weeks after the emperor's visit, the first session of the imperial Diet based on the new constitution opened. Japan's first general elections had been held the previous July, and three hundred representatives chosen by the people took their places in the parliamentary chamber. However, restricted in terms of both function and power, the parliament was by no means a democratic institution.

About that time, Iwao Oyama began to think about resigning from the post of minister of war. The bitter experience of fighting against his own cousin during the Satsuma Rebellion in 1877 had left him convinced that a soldier should not interfere in politics, and in May 1891, after eleven years' service, he submitted his resignation to Prime Minister Masayoshi Matsukata. Matsukata accepted it on the condition that Oyama agree to become the fifth taisho (general) in the army, following Takamori Saigo, two imperial princes, and Aritomo Yamagata. Oyama was not off the political scene for long, however. In March of the following year he was again appointed to the position of minister of war, this time in the second Ito cabinet.

After the conclusion of the Tientsin Treaty with China in 1885, Japan's position on the Korean peninsula was considerably weakened. The Chinese looked as if they wanted complete suzerainty over the region, and the Japanese government felt certain that it was only a matter of time before Japan was drawn into a conflict with its giant neighbor. It therefore wanted Oyama—one of the great pillars of the Meiji military establishment—back in the cabinet, to assist the nation in the event of such a crisis.

NOBUKO'S WEDDING

The spring of 1893 was a happy one for the Oyama family, apart from the hint of dark clouds gathering in the direction of the Korean peninsula. The eldest daughter, Nobuko, was engaged. Her fiancé was the Viscount Yataro Mishima, the first son of a former chief of police and Satsuma man. Yataro had only just returned from America but had already landed a post at the Ministry of Agriculture.

The pair were married on April 24. The fresh-faced bride, who had just turned seventeen, wore a wedding kimono sewn from material the empress had presented to her two years previously. As they gathered to see off the excited Nobuko, no one in the Oyama household could have guessed that she would be sent back to them a few months later, suffering from tuberculosis.

That winter a devastating strain of influenza swept through Tokyo, and poor Nobuko, with scarcely time to settle into her new married life, worked without rest to look after her husband's sick family. Inevitably she was infected herself, and the influenza played havoc on lungs already weakened by pleurisy as a child. Nobuko retired to bed in a serious state.

The Mishimas sent the young bride back home to rest in the hope that her condition would improve; on the advice of a doctor who suspected tuberculosis, Nobuko also spent time recuperating at the home of relatives in Yokosuka, outside of Tokyo.

In the new year, however, the Oyamas received word that the Mishimas wanted a divorce. Tuberculosis, as an incurable illness, was greatly feared, and the groom's family felt that in order for the family name to continue, they must force the young couple to

divorce and then find another, healthier bride. The feelings of
Nobuko and her husband did not come into consideration.

A letter written by Yataro Mishima to Sutematsu describes the
young man's dilemma at being caught between his family and his
beloved wife.

November 22

Dear Mrs. Oyama,

My humblest apologies for not being in touch with you
for so long. I have been wanting to visit you, but have been ill
and as the medicine appears to be having no effect have been
too weak to leave my bed.

I heard that Nobuko has gone to Yokosuka—it is warm
there and she will be with Aunt Ijichi and the Sameshimas, so
I am glad that she is not lonely.

Since the news that Nobuko and I will most likely have to
split I have been in the depths of despair, and spend every day
depressed and lethargic. Because I am responsible for taking
care of my family, my own opinions have no importance, and
after stating my wish I have left the matter entirely to my relatives. My sadness goes without saying, but must be nothing
compared to that of Nobuko.

I know it seems a cowardly excuse, but I believe that this
misfortune must be the result of something bad which I did
in a previous life. Please understand how terrible and sad I
feel about it.

When I am better I would like to pay a visit to you and
talk everything over in person. Once again, my apologies for
being so tardy in writing.

Yours sincerely,
Yataro

P.S. Please give my regards to General Oyama and the rest of
the family.

Meanwhile, Umeko had returned from the United States and was back teaching at the Peeresses' School. Having heard from Sutematsu about the tragedy of Nobuko's probable divorce, she rushed to speak with Yataro, incensed that he could even consider such a move. Whatever his mother's opinion, Umeko insisted, he simply could not just throw Nobuko out. It angered both Sutematsu and Umeko that a man educated at an American university could acquiesce so readily to his mother's wishes about his own marriage, even if it was "for the sake of the family."

Nobuko had no idea that her husband's family was pressing for a divorce, and continued to write to him frequently from Yokosuka. Servants intercepted and burned every one of those letters before they left the Sameshimas' home, as well as the letters Yataro sent. It was only by accident that Nobuko learned the truth, when a new maid passed on one of Yataro's letters to her by mistake. In it he had written that he must give up on the marriage for the sake of his family, and she should do the same. Nobuko, who had been looking forward to returning to her husband, received such a shock that her condition worsened considerably. Upon hearing of his daughter's deterioration, Iwao Oyama brought her back to the family home in Onden, Tokyo. Nobuko still hoped that it was all a bad dream, but upon arriving home to see the things she had taken to her husband's house as a bride stacked up near the entrance hall, the truth sank in. She collapsed, crying out in despair. After witnessing that scene, little Tomeko vowed that she would never marry. She remained single until the age of twenty-one, when she would have been considered almost too old to marry.

The Oyamas built a special room for Nobuko's convalescence. Sutematsu insisted on separate quarters for Nobuko to prevent the younger children from becoming infected, but at the time, little was known about tuberculosis in Japan and many who did not understand why Sutematsu was forcing Nobuko to live apart from the family cast her in the role of wicked stepmother. As far as Sutematsu was concerned, she was simply putting to practical use what she had learned at nursing school in New Haven. Sutematsu's greatest fear was infection, and she was diligent almost to the point of paranoia regarding the sterilization of everything Nobuko had touched. On one occasion, Tomeko went to see her sick older sister and was given a beautiful make-up brush. Sutematsu took it when she saw it, telling Tomeko that she would look after it. Ignorant of the danger of infection, the young girl grew angry with Sutematsu for taking the present. She saw it as proof that, as she and her speculating schoolfriends had suspected, she was not really Sutematsu's daughter. Thus Sutematsu's well-intentioned actions had an unfortunate negative repercussion.

Nobuko received the very best of care: Sutematsu cooked nutritious meals and made sure the girl spent time outside whenever the weather allowed. Gradually, Nobuko's condition improved until she was able to read poetry, and on her better days, she practiced penmanship by copying sections from her favorite novels.

Nobuko and Yataro's divorce was finalized in September 1895. Three months earlier, Iwao, Sutematsu, and Nobuko had gone on their first family holiday together. The Sino-Japanese War, which had broken out the previous year, had just ended, and General Oyama, fresh from a victorious command of the Second Army, now faced the unpleasant task of conveying the news of the finalized divorce to his daughter. Nobuko herself already knew what had happened, but appeared happy and relaxed as she toured Ise Shrine and the temples of Kyoto and Nara with her parents. Yet less than a year later, on May 21, 1896, her short life of twenty years drew to a close.

SCANDAL

The family had hardly begun to recover from the death of Nobuko when a novel that was to cause them a great deal of anguish appeared on the market. The author was Roka Tokutomi, brother of Soho Tokutomi, founder of the *Kokumin Shinbun* (*Peo-*

ple's Paper). The novel, *Hototogisu*, was serialized in that newspaper from the end of 1898 until May the following year. The plot involved a young woman named Namiko who contracts tuberculosis and is forced to divorce her beloved husband, Takeo. Namiko slowly fades away, dying broken-hearted. The book was firmly in the tear-jerker genre and not particularly well written, but the public sympathized with Namiko and her cries of "I want to live . . . a thousand years . . . ten thousand years!" and "Woe is me! Why was I born woman?" The book became a bestseller, running to one hundred printings over a ten-year period.

The inspiration for Tokutomi's novel came from conversations he had had with the wife of Iwao Oyama's aide-de-camp. In a foreword to the hundredth edition, he stated that "only the following events in the novel are based on fact: Namiko's divorce due to her tuberculosis, her husband Takeo's misery, Lieutenant Kataoka's angry retrieval of his daughter, the building of special quarters for the sick girl, the holiday trip with the family, and the return of funeral flowers sent by the Kawashima family."

Yet the novel's characters were undeniably based on the Oyama family. The author describes the character of Lieutenant Kataoka: "His corpulent body weighed about two hundred pounds, and even an Arab courser would be likely to sweat under him. . . . His eyes, however, out of harmony to the rest of his body, were narrow like those of an elephant, and mild to look upon. There was also a smile lurking constantly about his mouth, giving a humorous cast to his countenance." There could be no doubt in the minds of readers that "Kataoka" was a thinly disguised version of Iwao Oyama.

Kataoka's second wife Shigeko was described as "the daughter of a noted Choshu samurai," who "had been in London so long that a better English scholar was seldom to be found in Japan." Furthermore, she "had a fringe curled and divided in two over her high forehead," and her eyes were "large, and slightly turned up at the corners, with a hint of danger; her skin was dark and powdered, and her teeth gleamed white from brushing with care." A curled fringe was Sutematsu's trademark. She had worn the style since her New Haven days and continued to do so until the death of her husband. No matter how much Tokutomi protested that his book was fiction, the majority of readers would have seen the wife of General Oyama in the character of Shigeko.

What damaged Sutematsu most was the fact that Shigeko was painted as a cold and calculating stepmother who mistreated her husband's daughter Namiko.

"The sorrow Nami felt at her mother's death was too deep-seated for a child of eight, yet who could doubt that she would bloom into a lovely flower if the kindly light of the sun should shine upon her. When she met her stepmother,—the large mouth, the eyes somewhat oblique, the hair dressed in a foreign style, and the costume overperfumed,—she was naturally a little shy at first.

"But gently Nami would easily have been won over had not the stepmother been strangely prejudiced against the little child. Being devoid of tact, selfish, pedantic, and somewhat disagreeable, she treated her, a simple and artless child of eight or nine, as if she were a full-grown girl. The poor child was always left alone to feel how sad and cold the world was."

Tomeko also made an appearance in the novel, as the precocious younger daughter, "Komako." Occasionally Tomeko would read an episode of the serial in the *Kokumin Shinbun*, and would think how incredible it was that another family should have lives so similar to those of her own. It was not until she received a copy of the book from her older sister Fuyuko, with strict instructions never to show it to Sutematsu, that Tomeko realized on whom exactly the story was based. Reading it, she was hurt and angered by the depiction of Sutematsu as a thoroughly disagreeable mother.

Sutematsu had difficulty with written Japanese all her life, so it is doubtful that she ever read the novel, but the gossip and slanderous comments of those who believed the contents of the book to be true reached her ears. As the Japanese proverb says, "The nail that sticks up is knocked down," and Japanese society does not take kindly to those who have experienced something different, or who have special ability, particularly if they are female. With the *Hototogisu* incident Sutematsu was once again reminded of that fact, and it was many years before she completely recovered from the humiliation caused by the novel.

In the winter of 1920 the magazine *Fujokai* (*Women's World*) ran a feature article entitled "The Truth about *Hototogisu*," which explained what had actually happened between the Mishima and Oyama families. The characters of Namiko's stepmother and mother-in-law had been drawn "in an exaggerated fashion, in order to gain the sympathy of the reader for Namiko's plight," the article said, and expressed the editor's own sympathy for "these two women [Sutematsu and Mrs. Mishima], who are still living with the humiliation." Sutematsu cried when she read the article and commented that "Nobu was the loveliest girl you could ever meet, and I'm sure that if she were alive, she would have sympathized with me, knowing how much pain I've suffered from this whole affair.

A New English School
For Girls

PERSUADING ALICE

*E*ven amidst the *Hototogisu* scandal Sutematsu never forgot her commitment to women's education. Although marriage to Iwao Oyama had made her put aside her dreams of teaching, Sutematsu felt it was her duty and responsibility to use what influence she had as the wife of a high government official to contribute in other ways.

Since her New Haven days, Sutematsu had had absolute faith in Alice Bacon's ability as an educator, and had felt dissatisfied that Alice had been at the Peeresses' School for only a year. Wanting Alice to settle in Japan for a while, she went to speak with Hideo Takamine, principal of the Women's Higher Normal School. She wrote to Alice:

> I have been wanting to write to you for a long time, but before the New Year you know how busy all housewives are

in Japan and besides I wanted something definite to tell you about your prospects in case you decide to come. . . . He [Takamine, principal of the Women's Higher Normal School] came to see me this afternoon and we had a long conversation about it. It seems he wants just such a person as you for the school and he and Dr. Nakajima who teaches metaphysics there besides his work at the University had been talking about engaging an American lady of right kind, the only trouble being a want of sufficient funds to call her from such a distance. Now they have a fairer prospect of getting more money from Mombusho [the Ministry of Education], though not as much as they wish, still enough to engage another teacher. I am afraid that the salary is not high, but if you do not care for money part so much as the work[,] which will be most interesting in Japan as that school is the highest in Japan . . . I think the salary will be about one hundred yen a month, which is not very large from American point of view, but I think that will be the highest the school can afford, though Mr. Takamine did not say definitely what he can offer you, but I inferred from what he said as much. He said, however, that would such a person as you come so far on such a small salary as one hundred.

As to travelling expense he said clearly the school could *not* pay. Now you can consider about the matter and let me know if these terms are sufficient inducements for you to come. Moreover Mr. Takamine said if you wish to establish a school of your own after you have stayed a while, he thought he could help you in many ways. . . . He and Dr. Nakajima are very anxious to have more foreign ideas instilled into the school and for this a person of highest education and culture is needed who will be willing to work with them to this end. . . . You know Mr. Takamine stands foremost among the educationalists of Japan and I have more respect and admiration for him than for anyone else. . . . I am sure that if Ume

were here she would persuade you also. . . . Ume will come
back in May and will be here in case you decide to come during the summer. I miss her very much but I am glad she is
having such an opportunity to see England and all the famous
places. She deserves to have a good time now, for her life in
Japan is one continual work of some kind or other. I hope
she will come back strong and ready for more work.

Well, I hope you will be able to come. I am sure you will
be welcomed by many people whom you left as your warm
friends.

(January 7, 1899)

Takamine was of the same Aizu origins as Sutematsu and had
been a classmate of her brother Kenjiro at Nisshinkan. After studying history and economics at Keio Gijuku (now Keio University),
Takamine had gone to work for the Ministry of Education, which
immediately sent him to Oswego Normal School in New York
State. From 1875 to 1878 he observed American teacher training
and reported on it to his superiors. Sutematsu was in New Haven
at that time and knew Takamine well, having met him through her
brother.

Takamine believed that education encompassed not only lessons
learned in the classroom but also what the instructor and students
could learn from each other in everyday life. To this end he wanted Alice to live on campus as well as teach so that the girls could
come into regular contact with her.

After years of following retrogressive policies toward women's
education, the government in 1899 finally recognized the value of
higher education for females. One of two laws it promulgated was
concerned with higher education for girls (Act of Girls' High
Schools). The law, which required every prefecture to have at least
one institution of higher learning for females funded out of public
money, naturally brought about a sudden increase in the number
of girls' schools. Until that time education for women had been

mainly left to the private schools established by missionaries in the early years of the Meiji period. Women's Higher Normal School was the only higher-level institution for women. Sutematsu had watched the developments in women's education over the years and, predicting a sudden rise in the number of girls' schools, wanted Alice to train the future teachers of those schools.

Sutematsu's impassioned request that she come to Japan in the summer of that same year was a little too sudden for Alice, and she asked her Japanese sister to wait until the following year. As principal of the Hampton Normal School, Alice had responsibilities that prevented her from uprooting herself and going to Japan on such short notice. Sutematsu wrote,

> It is nearly three weeks since Mr. Takamine asked me to write to you, but you know I have been nearly standing on my head with my daughter's trousseau, for she is to be married in June. Mr. Takamine will wait for you till next year if it is impossible for you to come this year. . . . I am afraid it is almost impossible to make you understand the difficulties which stand in Mr. Takamine's way in regard to managing that school, for though he is at the head of the school, he is under the Mombusho (Educational Department) which again is dependent on the Diet for its budget. As every year the budget to be placed before the Diet changes according to circumstances, we never can tell what may happen next year. Mr. Takamine took a long time to consider whether he could safely say that he would wait for you, not that he was unwilling, (because the kind of help that he hoped to get from you is one that he is in no hurry [sic] and is one that requires time to bring to fruition) but he was afraid that when you get here he may not be able to pay you your salary on account of cutting down the Mombusho budget. Now however, he seems able to see his way clear and said definitely that he would wait.
>
> You see Japanese education is dependent on politics, and if

the government changes, the head of Mombusho changes, and if a cranky old conservative happens to be the Minister of Education, the heads of different schools naturally will come to clash with him and resignations, suspended work and general hubbub follows.

When you get here you will understand all the difficulties that stand in the way of our educationalists. Still Mr. Takamine is such an able man that Mombusho will not be able to find another to displace him even if their ideas come to collision. So I think you may safely place yourself in Mr. Takamine's hands and I am sure so long as he takes a thing in hand he will carry it through thick and thin. . . .

Well, I will write again when I am through with the wedding festivities, and when my head is more cleared and can contain other matters besides trousseaus, go-betweens, feasts and presents. Have you seen Ume? I hope she will persuade you to come.

(May 25, 1899)

As Sutematsu's comment suggests, Umeko Tsuda was in the United States at the time. Chosen to be the Japanese representative to travel to Denver, Colorado for a conference of the International Congress of the Federation of Women's Clubs, Umeko took leave from her teaching posts at the Peeresses' School and Women's Higher Normal School to enjoy her third trip across the Pacific.

After the conference Umeko traveled to Washington, where she met Adeline Lanman, her host mother and a friend to all five of those young girls who had arrived from Japan twenty-seven years before. Now an elderly widow, Mrs. Lanman was moved to tears upon seeing her Japanese daughter standing before her, representing the fight of Japanese women for equal education. Instead of returning to Japan that autumn as scheduled, Umeko accepted an invitation from distinguished English acquaintances to visit their country. She made the most of the first free time she had enjoyed in many years by sitting in on English literature lectures at Oxford University and visiting an old Bryn Mawr College friend living in France.

From Europe, Umeko returned to the United States not, as she had planned, to Japan. She told Alice that she was finally going to realize her long-held dream of opening her own school for training English teachers, and that she would be extremely grateful if Alice would agree to assist her. Umeko had cherished the idea of a school since her Bryn Mawr days, and it was not the first time she had brought the matter up with Alice: they had discussed it when Umeko spent a summer at Alice's home in Hampton, Virginia, helping her to write her book *Japanese Girls and Women*. Urged by both Sutematsu and Umeko to return to Japan, Alice finally gave in to the wishes of her two old friends and began to prepare for her second trip across the Pacific.

A BEGINNING

Umeko returned to Japan at the end of July, 1899. On hearing Umeko's latest news, Sutematsu quickly dashed off a letter to Alice.

> I was very glad to hear about you and my other friends on the other side of the Pacific through Ume and hearing her talk seemed to bring back all my American experience anew. I could imagine what you are doing this summer, though the Holderness of the present must be so different from that of the time I knew.
>
> There is one thing which makes me rather uneasy. Ume seems to think you will be disappointed with your work here when you come, for she says your work in America is done so quickly and so successfully that you will find every thing here so slow and the result so imperceptible. Please do not be very sanguine, but rather come with the idea that you hope to accomplish something by taking a long time about it, and that something not a great deal, either. You know Japan has not

changed very much since you were here, in fact, in some things we have gone back and you will find everything just as slow and as conventional as ever. But I dare say Ume has given you a faithful picture of the present day and you are sufficiently prepared with all our deficiencies. The only change you will notice will be in the faces of your friends. The young children that you knew are now quite grown up and the young people of old are now married and some of them have children of their own and the middle aged people that you remember are grown old and white haired.

My children are growing very fast and in proportion, I suppose I am growing old. My husband grows fatter every year and I thinner. We two are the only ones left in Tokyo. I have sent my children to Numazu [the Oyama country home one hundred miles west of Tokyo] with my sister in law, and we shall not be able to join them for some days yet. . . .

My husband was not able to get away from Tokyo on account of some military business that had to be attended to, but as soon as that is over, we hope to spend three or four weeks in Numazu. You see he has been made the Chief of the Staff and everything connected with the army must come up to him. It is a great nuisance. He did not want to take up the office, after two years of leisure and he turned deaf ear to every persuasion but when the Emperor commanded, he could not very well refuse unless he gave up his sword and uniform. So he has to work again in this hot weather and you can see the life of soldier is not very easy in Japan, though not quite so hard as some of your soldiers at present, who are ordered to the Philippines and have to fight not only with men, but with dreadful fevers. . . .

It is too hot to write any more. I shall write again from Numazu. My kind regards to any people that I know who happen to be with you.

(August 5, 1899)

Even after his retirement from the post of minister of war in 1896, Iwao Oyama still wielded a great deal of influence in his position as elder statesman, although he had little to do with the day-to-day running of the ministry. In 1898 he was awarded the position of Supreme Military Councilor, along with three other people, and his title was upgraded from count to marquis. Soon after, Oyama began a new and relatively easy job: supervising the officials in charge of educating the crown prince, Yoshihito. When the crown prince was staying at the imperial villa at Numazu, Oyama would invite him to the Oyama's summer house nearby, and the young man soon became fond of his generous father-like host.

The Oyama house at Numazu may still be seen. Although not in the condition it once was in, it provides the visitor with an idea of what it might have been like a hundred years ago. Iwao and Sutematsu loved the house surrounded by pine trees, and for many years enjoyed a marvelous view of the nearby ocean. In Numazu the winters are warm, and a cool sea breeze takes the edge off the summer heat: the perfect climate for the family's health. Their fourth daughter, Hisako, was a particularly sickly child, and spent most of her school holidays there.

May 1899 brought the untimely death of General Soroku Kawakami, chief of the General Staff and a trusted colleague of Oyama, who was ordered to replace him. Under normal circumstances, the government would not have gone to the extreme of an imperial order to force Oyama, out of military life since the Sino-Japanese War, to command the armed forces, but the tension-filled situation on the continent demanded the strength and experience that only he could provide. Oyama reluctantly entered the military mainstream again. He was fifty-eight years old, and Sutematsu was forty.

In 1895 Russia, along with Germany and France, began to press Japan to return the Liaotung Peninsula to China. The peninsula had been taken during the Sino-Japanese War, and now those three nations claimed that Japan's presence there disturbed the peace in Asia. What came to be known as the Tripartite Intervention took place directly after the signing of the Shimonoseki Peace Treaty. Japan, too weak militarily and economically to argue, had no choice but to give in to the three nations' demand. Russia went on in 1898 to lease Port Arthur and Dairen from the Chinese for a period of twenty-five years, ostensibly to protect its neighbor from foreign invasion, although a more likely motivation was the Russians' desire to acquire land for the completion of the Trans-Siberian Railway. The Japanese saw the move as an aggressively expansionist one, particularly when they had just gained a foothold in Manchuria themselves, and the nation prepared itself for what seemed an inevitable conflict. Following the death of Soroku Kawakami, the government considered Iwao Oyama the only man capable of steering the nation through such a military crisis.

Alice Bacon arrived in Japan for the second time in April 1900. A new century had begun, and Sutematsu, Umeko, and Alice hoped it would signal the start of a new era for women's education in Japan. At the ages of forty-one, thirty-seven, and forty-two respectively, they were as excited as young girls at the prospect of fulfilling the dream they had shared for many years.

That July Umeko resigned from her teaching posts at the Peeresses' School and Women's Higher Normal School and began to prepare for the opening of the new English teachers' school. Alice assisted when she was free from her work at the Women's Higher Normal School. Umeko had always believed that if women were to improve their status they would first have to become economically self-reliant, and to this end hoped that the girls who attended her school would eventually go out into society as English teachers. In addition, eating and sharing accommodation with their instructors would hopefully provide the girls with a more international outlook.

Located in a small Japanese house near the imperial palace, the Joshi Eigakujuku opened its doors on September 14, 1900. The staff consisted of Umeko as director, Sutematsu as advisor, and three teachers, Alice, Hikoichiro Sakurai, who had recently returned from a study tour of women's educational institutions in the United States and was a friend of Umeko's father, and Mitsuko Watanabe, a young woman whom Alice had adopted and taken back to America on her previous trip. A total of seventeen people were present at the opening ceremony that day including those five, other staff, guests, and students.

Umeko began her inaugural speech to the small gathering in the "assembly hall," a ten-mat room (about 180 square feet). While the school needed to improve its facilities, she said, as director she was confident that the enthusiasm of the teaching staff combined with the willingness of the pupils to learn would ensure its success. Although the stated aim of the school was to produce female English teachers, the staff would encourage the girls to cultivate interests in other fields, as well as womanly qualities, in order that they might develop as well-rounded individuals.

Alice's contributions to the school were tremendous. She worshiped with pupils in the hall every morning and taught them to read the Bible and sing hymns. In addition, she conducted a lesson in current affairs every Friday in her own living room. To save the school's meager finances, Alice asked no money for her two years at the school, and payed Umeko rent out of her salary from the Women's Higher Normal School. Prior to leaving America Alice had formed a fundraising committee among friends of Sutematsu and Umeko, and when the school became overcrowded and had to relocate six months after its founding, it was through the good offices of that committee that Umeko obtained another house, in nearby Motozonocho.

When Alice's two-year stay was completed in April 1902, the educator returned to the United States, having guided the school to a firm footing. She and Sutematsu continued to exchange voluminous amounts of correspondence over the years, but they were never to see each other in person again.

SUPPORT FROM ABROAD

Umeko's school continued to flourish, and by 1902 the number of students had grown from ten to thirty, too many for the Motozonocho site to accommodate. That summer Umeko bought a house and section of land behind the British Legation for ten thousand yen. Were it not for a generous donation from a Mrs. Woods of Boston, the school could not have afforded such a large purchase. The two yen that each girl paid monthly was swallowed up almost entirely by salaries and food, and the school relied on donations for renovations and classroom equipment.

Sutematsu, for her part, decided to ask her old Vassar classmates for assistance. It was twenty years since their graduation, and the members of the class of 1882 were about to publish a special alumnae magazine edition to commemorate their anniversary. Sutematsu's letter to the secretary of the class of 1882 was included.

> Your letter has made me go back to the times twenty years ago, and while the iron is hot, I must strike off a few lines. But you must not regard this as a classletter, for my English is getting so rusty from want of practice that I dare not write anything that might be read before so many people. Just tell the class that I am living and send them a hearty greeting. Speaking of English, perhaps you will be interested to hear that English is the one most spoken among our foreign languages in Japan, and ever since the Anglo-Japanese alliance, it seems to have given an additional impetus to its study. And the best school for English is the little school for girls which Miss Tsuda started with the help of Miss Bacon two years ago, and I am its humble adviser. . . . If you should hear of anyone who is interested in the school, I wish you would speak about it, for it is doing an immense amount of good, and try to get a little money for it, because it is in need of funds and even a few hundred dollars would help enormously. The school has

been growing ever since it started, and now it has eighty-five pupils. Miss Tsuda has applications all the time, but she has to refuse them on account of her limited accommodations. Carrie Macadam, who is here in Japan, now teaches about two or three hours a week. If you care to hear more about it, I shall be glad to give you any information, or Miss Bacon who has now returned to America. As for myself, what can I say that will be of interest to you? Absolutely nothing. My life, compared with yours, is so uneventful. Yesterday, since I received your letter, I met an American friend of mine and asked her what she thought would interest you who are on the other side of the Pacific, and she said, 'O, anything about your daily life, what you do, how you spend your time.' But do you care to hear why I discharged one of my servants, or that I have engaged new ones, or that I have had some military officers to dinner who talked shop all the time, or that my youngest boy was very stupid at lessons and I lost my patience, or that my silk worms which I am rearing are not doing well on account of the cold weather, or that I am bothered out of my life with all sorts of societies, clubs and associations which send me letters by reams, etc., etc.? No, that kind of story is the same all over the world and in that respect I don't think my life is different from that of the average American woman. As I have nothing interesting to say, and besides the mail goes this afternoon, I better stop and send you my photograph to apologize for all my sins of omission. Please write again after the meeting, and tell me all the particulars. I hoped to send you my children's photograph, but I cannot find any. My daughter is getting quite grown up. She is taller than I am, which you know in Japan is remarkable.

P.S.—My spelling is all out of gear. I trust you can make out my words.

Twenty years after graduation, Sutematsu's class managed to

raise a thousand dollars for its alma mater. Another fifty dollars was raised for the English school that one of its members served as an advisor of. Fifty dollars was hardly enough to relieve the school's financial crisis, but Umeko was grateful for the effort made by Sutematsu's former classmates. Sutematsu wrote to the class secretary, "I must thank you most sincerely for such a generous gift, and will you kindly convey my heart-felt thanks to all the members of our class. I enclose Miss Tsuda's receipt together with her letter to me, to show you how the money is to be used. I think her letter will tell you far more than anything I can write about it, and so, though it is written very hastily and intended for my eye alone, I think it would be better to let you see it for yourself.— *Stematz Oyama*."

Umeko's letter (following) and a receipt written in Japanese were included in the commemorative issue of the alumnae magazine.

41 Niotozono Cho [*sic*], Tokyo, Sept. 1, 1902.

My Dear Stematz:

Knowing that you were out of the city, I have delayed in sending you the enclosed receipt for the most kind gift from your classmates. It is a very unexpected gift, and comes at a most opportune time. You know that I am obliged to enlarge the school this fall, as the school-room accommodations are utterly inadequate to having eighty-five and more girls in the classes. In our new building I have several new rooms. May this $50.00 be used in school furniture? I must get teachers' desks and chairs and will need fully this sum in September, before school opens. I think your friends would prefer the money used for something permanent of this kind, and $50 —100 yen of our money—will just about furnish two of our school rooms. To tell you the truth, I was wondering how I could get the rooms furnished, and this gift is most opportune. I think it very kind of these friends to send it, and I appreciate their kind thought, realizing, of course, that for your sake and your interest in the school it was done. Besides the formal receipt, will you convey to them my warmest thanks and tell them about this use of the money. You only too well know all our needs, so I will not have to go over the facts with you, but will you tell your friends how much our girls need in every way, and how hard it is to give them all we want to. It is the same struggle as in the old days in America and other lands, when women wanted something higher and better than what they had given them, and the friends who were working were hampered in many ways.

In February 1903 the new buildings were completed, and students were able to study in something resembling an educational institution for the first time since the school's opening. Umeko's school had come a long way, thanks to the generosity of benefactors both in Japan and America, who had raised approximately eleven thousand yen over a three-year period. In actual fact, to Japan's shame, ninety percent of the funds were donated from abroad—something that has changed little over the intervening hundred years to the present day, when the country's seeming reluctance to give money for educational and cultural activities is frequently attacked by other nations, and belies its status as an economic giant.

On April 2 of that year, the school's first graduation ceremony was held, and Sutematsu spoke a few words to each of the eight new graduates on behalf of the school. It was a small beginning, but Umeko and Sutematsu felt that their determination of twenty years to do something for the improvement of women's education was actually having an effect on Japanese society.

The Russo-Japanese War

THE FIELD MARSHAL'S WIFE

While Sutematsu was preoccupied with Umeko's school, her husband was embroiled in an approaching military crisis.

Since its defeat at the hands of Japan, the "sleeping lion," as the Chinese empire was known, had been caught up in a struggle among the great powers for hegemony of its lands. Not surprisingly, the tide of antiforeign sentiment was rapidly rising in China, and riding the crest of the wave of xenophobia were the Boxers with their slogan of "save China and destroy the West." Throughout the country they promoted the violent expulsion of all foreign nationals, and in May 1900 attacked the foreign legations in Peking in what later became known as the Boxer Rebellion. In July troops from Japan, Russia, France, Britain, Germany, Austria, and the United States combined to put down the rebellion, succeeding in mid-August. The Boxer Rebellion was Iwao Oyama's first overseas conflict since his appointment as chief of staff. It was also the first time Japanese troops had combined with those of Western nations in a common cause, and the soldiers' discipline and bravery attracted the admiring attention of the great powers.

The Japanese government had learned from its bitter experience after the war with China that rather than conduct an independent foreign policy, it was far more efficient to ally itself with either Russia or Britain to fulfill its objectives in Manchuria and Korea. Prime Minister Hirobumi Ito and others favored recognizing Russia's rights in Manchuria, if in return the Russians would acknowledge Japan's in Korea; however, the first Katsura cabinet, which formed in June 1901, took a different view and decided to negotiate an agreement with the British. The ensuing talks resulted in the Anglo-Japanese Alliance, signed in January 1902 by the British foreign minister Landsdowne and the Japanese minister Hayashi. Japan was to help protect British rights in China, while Britain would do the same for Japan in China and Korea. Britain also promised to remain neutral should Japan and Russia be drawn into a conflict. The Alliance administered a serious blow to Russia's expansionist visions in Asia, and relations with Japan steadily worsened.

Twenty years earlier Sutematsu had delivered a stirring speech at her commencement on relations between Japan and Britain— never did she imagine that the empire that refused to recognize Japan as an independent nation would one day be entering into an equal agreement with its government.

Iwao Oyama was having a quiet time in his role as chief of staff—he felt too old for the job and left most of the daily tasks to his younger men. On the dot of four every afternoon, the general packed up his belongings and went either straight home or to the house of his newlywed daughter Tomeko. In 1900 Tomeko had married Chiharu Watanabe, son of an Imperial Household Department minister. The world is a small place, and the president of the Bank of Japan where Chiharu worked was none other than Yataro

Mishima, Tomeko's deceased sister's ex-husband. On one occasion Tomeko received a call informing her that the president of the Bank of Japan would be coming by for a brief visit. The last person she expected to see was Yataro Mishima. He deposited a diamond ring with the astonished Tomeko and left, saying, "My, Tomeko, how you've grown! This is a memento of your sister." Nobuko had sent her most treasured ring to Yataro when they parted. Tomeko's attitude softened considerably toward the Mishima family after that incident.

On the days when Iwao Oyama visited his daughter, a telephone call in the afternoon would inform her that "His Excellency will be visiting." Tomeko would open the shutters at the back of the house, and sure enough her father would soon appear, meandering through the garden, stopping here and there to admire a particular flower or tree. After drinking a cup of tea on the wooden veranda of the house, the general would leave as quietly as he had come, with the words, "I'll come again soon, look after yourself now." Oyama in his sixties had experienced the mellowing of character that often comes with age, and it was said that "his presence engendered in those around him the kind of warmth associated with a spring wind."

Yet, with the signing of the Anglo-Japanese Alliance and the accompanying heightening of tension on the continent, Oyama could no longer afford to spend much time with his daughter or indeed with any of the rest of his family. By 1903, public opinion was strongly in favor of "quelling Russia."

Claiming a need to maintain law and order, Russia refused to withdraw its troops after the Boxer Rebellion and effectively occupied Manchuria. Unhappy about the situation, in April 1902 Japan, Britain, and the United States forced Russia to promise it would withdraw its troops in three stages, the last stage to be completed by October of that year. The first group was withdrawn as agreed, but the second movement of troops was suddenly cancelled. Instead, Russia increased the size of its force in the area, fanning out as far as the border with Korea. In addition, the Russian government made demands of China that seemed to completely ignore China's territorial rights and open-door policy.

The Japanese saw China and Korea as important markets and sources of raw material, and the public outcry against Russia's arrogance soon turned into a call for Japan to preserve peace in the area, even if strong-arm tactics became necessary.

Beginning in the summer of 1903, the Japanese foreign minister Jutaro Komura held several rounds of talks with the Russian minister Rosen in Tokyo. Although the Japanese made a number of concessions, Russia refused to alter its stance on Manchuria, and when Japan presented its final proposal on January 13, 1904, the Russians delayed giving an answer, instead moving troops into the Yalu River area and expelling all Japanese nationals from Vladivostok. Realizing that nothing more could be gained from negotiation, Japan cut off diplomatic relations with Russia on February 6 and declared war on February 10.

Not long before war broke out Tomeko's husband was transferred to London, and she went to her parents' home to say goodbye to the family. There she found her father sitting among his long-neglected military clothing and trunks, patiently repairing them. Tomeko, like most other Japanese, was expecting a conflict with Russia in the near future, and she asked her father whether he was going off to war.

"Don't ask such a stupid question," he snapped in reply. "Do you really think they're going to send an old man of sixty-three like me into battle? But a soldier has to be prepared to fight any time, that's the only reason I'm repairing this gear."

Oyama did not wish to worry his daughter, who was about to go abroad, but military secrecy also prevented him from telling even those closest to him about the imminent conflict. It was several months later as she was crossing the Pacific Ocean that Tomeko discovered her father had been appointed by the emperor to be commander-in-chief of the Japanese army in Manchuria.

In the following letter Sutematsu describes to Alice the circumstances surrounding that appointment:

> It is such a long time since I have written to you. I suppose you think I have forgotten you. The truth is, I have got out of the habit of writing letters and my English is getting so rusty that I am really ashamed of myself, but if you do not mind my broken English and bad spelling I will tell you of that which is occupying my attention at this moment. I can not tell you of all that has occurred since I last wrote to you, because that was so long ago for one thing, and there have been many things that might interest you. But I have forgotten all about them, at least those things are over-shadowed in interest by the all absorbing topic of the present war.
>
> You must know we have been in the midst of it from the very beginning, which was in the earlier part of June. At that time the people did not think it was to be anything so serious as it has turned out to be, but I knew better, but of course then I did not think my husband would personally take command himself. It was on the third or fourth of June when I first heard of the trouble in Corea [sic]. In the morning a lot of army people came to our house (we were living at the official residence then, being before the great earthquake), and had a meeting. My husband said it was more convenient than at the office. Those meetings lasted for several days and then began the busy time for all. Sometimes my husband had people come as early as five in the morning, before he was up, and all day till late at night and then during the night he would be wakened several times by letters, telegrams and telephone messages.
>
> (October 28, 1904)

Oyama, who had suspected since his days as minister of war that a conflict with Russia was unavoidable, secretly felt that, although he was getting on in years, there was no one in the Japanese army better qualified for the task at hand. Naval minister Yamamoto asked him to stay in Japan and assist in plotting the nation's course from home, but the general refused.

"Here we have Ito, Yamagata, and Katsura to run things, so there is no need for me," Oyama replied. "But over there we have Kodama, Nogi, Kuroki, Kawamura, and Nozu, all great men in their own right, who will all want to do things their own way. I'm confident that I can use all of their various talents to maximum advantage and make them work together. I have to go."

General Gentaro Kodama, who had already been chosen for the position of chief of staff, admired Iwao Oyama and his methods and was adamant about having him on the battlefield. As Sutematsu often joked to her friends, "General Kodama is my husband's favorite, next is me, and third is steak." It would be no exaggeration to say that it was the combination of Oyama and Kodama that enabled Japan to emerge victorious from the conflict with Russia.

On the morning of July 6, Oyama posed for a photograph in the garden of his official residence with Sutematsu, his sons, Takashi and Kashiwa, and his daughter Hisako, before driving through streets thronged with well-wishers on the way to Shinbashi station to embark on his seventh expedition.

With her husband's departure Sutematsu turned to a flurry of activity, reclaiming the volunteer work spirit she had fostered all those years ago in New Haven. She threw herself into relief work for the Japan Red Cross Ladies' Volunteer Nursing Association and the Ladies' Patriotic Association established in 1901. Most of the women in those organizations were from the imperial and noble families and had never gone out of the house by themselves, let alone worked for money or a cause. Sutematsu was the only women in the upper class capable of efficiently organizing volunteer work, such as fundraising and the making of bandages at the Red Cross hospital.

With the outbreak of the Russo-Japanese War came an increase in the frequency of correspondence between Sutematsu and Alice. Sutematsu protested that her English had deteriorated, but in fact it was as excellent as ever, and her letters convey her enthusiasm about the activities of Japanese women on the home front during the conflict.

> In the meantime, people have not been idle. As soon as war was declared, all sorts of things, food, clothing, wine, foot-gear, paper, money—in fact, everything that is contained in Japanese life was sent to the Army and Navy. In July, a com-mittee of sixty ladies of which I was a member started to col-lect money among women & the result was a tremendous success, a part of which was spent in buying handkerchiefs to be sent to those who had already gone to the seat of war and the rest we have decided to put into the bank to be used whenever and in whatever way we thought best when the occasion demanded. . . . You had no idea—at least I can not half express to you—of the enthusiasm of the people and the way they offer everything they possess to afford comfort to the soldiers. . . . Then the ladies who belonged to the Red Cross Society go every day to the Hospital to make bandages. . . . We all wear nurses' costume and we carbolize our hands & clothes in a truly hospital style for the Army is very strict about antiseptic treatment and none of the bandages not made in the antiseptic way is received by the authorities. We have made millions of bandages but we are still making them. . . . So you see with all these things on my hands I have had no time for anything. All my relatives are more than active in the affair of the war. . . .
>
> (October 28, 1904)

Six days later she wrote to Alice again:

Today I went to see the formal opening of the kindergarten

of the Kuazoku Gakko [the Peers' School]. I dare say Ume has told you about it, at least about its beginning and how much she had to do for its existence. She told me that she received a letter from you in which you expressed so much concern for the welfare of Japan at this crisis and especially for us. Of course I feel much anxiety, but at the same time I know that we shall be victorious in the end, and my husband though he may suffer many privations still he will return after conquering China, all safe & well. There are moments however when we can not help taking a gloomy view on this matter. . . .

We are all waiting anxiously for a telegram from China to announce the taking of Port Arthur which you know is a very important place. If we take that of course our navy will never be hampered in its movements but can go into the Gulf of Pe Chili with perfect safety. . . .

(November 3, 1904)

Alice found herself swept along by Sutematsu's enthusiasm for the cause of Japanese victory and her relief work. She canvassed among her friends for money, which she sent across the Pacific.

It was only yesterday that I thought of you and thought of writing to you, for it is a long time since I wrote to you. It is good of you to give us so much and I can not tell you how grateful I am to you and to Mrs. Frank and Miss Bradley. Of course I shall write to them both and thank them for their generosity. I do not know how you wish me to spend the money. If you leave it to me, I am quite perplexed, for there is so much need of money in all sides that sometimes when people give me money to do what I like with, I don't know what to to. When I hear the tales of hardship that our soldiers are suffering at the front, I want to spend every cent I have to buy some comfort to send to the front; when I see the poor wounded and the sick looking so patient and so grateful for any favour received, then I want to do some thing for them; when I hear of little children and old people left behind to get along as well as they may in this cold weather with nothing but potatoes to eat, then I want to help them. In my waking hours I need not tell you that my thought is entirely engrossed with this war. I am not anxious about my husband in the ordinary sense, for thanks to his position he has all the comforts that he can have at such a time and in such a place. They give him the best of every thing, even before the Imperial Princess, and I have sent him every possible warm things [*sic*] and whenever I have a chance I send him some sort of food stuff which is transportable. But what I most feel for him is his mental strain, for his responsibility is so enormous that he has to bear the weight of it whether in victory or defeat. I am fortunate in having only my husband at the front, for so many women that I know have not only their husbands but two or three sons as well, and when one of these is killed, it seems to me the situation is unbearable. But they are brave, and I often wonder if I could be as brave if I had three there and if one of them were killed. The most trying thing that I have to do is to go on a visit of condolence to one of these families. Of course it is a great and glorious thing to die for one's country, but after all we are wives and mothers before we are patriots and who does not feel this natural sorrow, though the whole country may be resounding with the stories of his bravery and his glorious death. . . .

I wish you could be here now. Can't you become a correspondent of some paper? There is one thing that you could help us [with] immensely. If you hear of any body wishing to travel in Japan and yet gave it up on account of the war, will you tell such people there is no danger and Japan is as quiet as at any time, that every thing is the same. You know one of the revenues of this country is derived from globe trotters, who are generally wealthy people and spend a great deal of money buying silks, curios and other things. I hear there is a great falling off in the travellers to this country and consequently less money comes into the country. Of course that is a small matter, but still every little counts. . . . With many thanks for the money and ever so much love. . . .

(December 1–2, 1904)

Why did Sutematsu, who worked from morning until night on relief work and had no time to glance at a newspaper, use her precious spare moments to write these long detailed letters to Alice one after the other? Through correspondence with her American friend and confidante, Sutematsu hoped to convey her true thoughts and feelings about the war that, as the wife of the Supreme Commander General Oyama, she was unable to voice to other Japanese.

While on the one hand, the country's newspapers were full of stories describing the glorious deaths of brave Japanese troops, anti-war sentiment was also growing, as typified by Akiko Yosano's famous poem "Please don't die." Although the families with husbands and sons killed in the fighting were never far from Sutematsu's mind, as the wife of a commander-in-chief she could never let it be known that she put the love of her husband and children before that of her country. Sutematsu believed that Japan must win the war, in order that the deaths of tens of thousands of soldiers not be in vain, and to justify the war in which her husband was the supreme commander. She wanted Americans to know how unified in spirit the Japanese were and how determined a fight the tiny nation was putting up against Russia at home and on the battlefield.

Following the surrender of Port Arthur on New Year's Day in 1905 the Japanese army in Manchuria faced a battle—Mukden— that was crucial to the future of the nation. The government had been able to meet half the costs of the war by issuing war bonds in Britian, France, Germany, and the United States, but the conflict had already dragged on for a year, and Japan was finding itself in dire straits financially. If the war with Russia continued much longer, it was clear the country would go bankrupt. It was also clear that once the winter snows melted, enabling the Russians to send reinforcements, the Japanese army would be overwhelmed by vast numbers of fresh enemy troops. The only hope for victory therefore was a decisive win at Mukden followed by peace negotiations.

At the opening of the Mukden engagements, Russia had the advantage in terms of numbers: 360,000 troops to Japan's 250,000. Japan, however, had by far the better strategy, and it was that which led to eventual victory. The encirclement of Mukden by Oyama and Kodama caught the Russian general Kuropatkin by surprise, leading to a breakdown in his chain of command. The Russian forces were thrown into a state of confusion, and after several days of fierce fighting, Kuropatkin ordered his men to retreat. On March 10 the Japanese army achieved its second victory in the war.

TIES OF FRIENDSHIP

After the capture of Mukden, detailed articles concerning the Russo-Japanese War began to appear in American newspapers, lavishing praise on Iwao Oyama for his succession of victories against the mighty Russia. Without exception they proudly added that the commander's wife had been educated in the United States and was a graduate of Vassar.

Alice Bacon was unable to meet Sutematsu's request to go to Japan as a special correspondent, but she did find another way to assist her friends' war effort. She had observed that the accounts of Japan at war published in American newspapers were very different from the realities that Sutematsu and Shigeko Uryu described in their letters, so in an attempt to rectify the situation she began to publish those letters for American readers. The following article appeared in a New Haven paper:

LEADING JAPANESE WOMEN WRITE A TOUCHING STORY OF WAR TIME SACRIFICE

To the Editor of The Register, Sir:

Some letters from Japanese women have come to me within a few months which I am publishing in part, quite without the intention or consent of the writers, knowing that if the publication does any good to the Japanese cause, the offence will be forgiven me. The writers are of especial interest to us New Haveners, in that they both have in their girlhood called our city their home and are both more or less known to many of us. One of them, Marchioness Oyama, was for ten years a member of my father's family, and still thinks of New Haven as her American home, though she has not seen it for more than twenty years. She prepared for college at Hillhouse high school and after her graduation of Vassar in '83 [sic], took a short special course in the New Haven Training School for Nurses, returning to Japan in the autumn of the same year. There she soon married General Oyama, then minister of war, and now viceroy of Manchuria and commander-in-chief of the Japanese armies in the field.

My other correspondent came as a child to Fair Haven, where her home was in the family of the Rev. John S. G. Abbot. She too, after a course at Vassar, returned to her own country and married a young Japanese graduate of Annapolis, now Admiral Uriu under whose command the first shot in the war was fired at Chemuipo last February. These two women, intimate friends but in two distinct circles of Japanese society, have written to me rather fully, each opening a window into a life that is little known to Americans. . . .

Marchioness Oyama says:

"We are all very busy. Each of us is trying to do anything in his power to help on the war. You will be astonished to hear how all the women of the nobility who have always lived shut up in their houses have come out to do their share of the work. These ladies, who have not even known how to put on their own stockings, come to the Red Cross hospital without any attendants, with a bundle of regulation hospital dress in one hand, and a little box of luncheon in the other, dressed very plainly, looking for all the world like factory girls." (Perhaps this statement needs the explanation that at the hospital these noble ladies work all day under the surgeon's orders, preparing aseptic dressings to be sent out to the field.)

Marchioness Oyama continues:

"There is the Ladies' Patriotic Association, which looks after the families of the wounded and disabled, and another association which visits the families of the soldiers at the fronts. Then there is a group of ladies who are sewing the shirts of soldiers, and the money they get will be returned toward the war fund. I am connected with all of these, and besides I am one of a committee to collect funds to buy comforts to be sent to the men at the front. This last thing is what I started myself with a few of the army officers wives. . . .

"I assure you that the people are very earnest about this war, and they will not leave a stone unturned to bring it to a successful conclusion. From the emperor to the lowest coolie every Japanese will do his best, for it is not only the soldiers who can wage war to successful end. An army not backed by the people can never accomplish its object. And the moral support which America is giving is a tremendous factor in urging on this struggle."

Here we can see something of the cost of this terrible war to the gallant little nation that is fighting the battle of freedom for Asia, or life or death to itself. The letters from which I have quoted are in no sense appeals for aid. The Japanese, both men and women, are fighting this war alone and on their own responsibility, and ask no favors. But it seems to me that New Haveners should have a special interest in these two women and their work. Can we not show them that the old tie of association and affection that still binds them to New Haven binds us as well to them? Can we not, in the midst of our peace and prosperity, send to these trans-Pacific New Haven women a sign of our sympathy—a remembrance from their old home that they can use in whatever way seems best to them for the help of their country?

The names and positions of the two ladies will serve as vouchers for the right use of any subscriptions made to their work. That they are intelligent and earnest enough to use wisely whatever comes into their hands the letters themselves show. Any subscriptions sent to this paper, or to me personally, will be promptly acknowledged and transmitted to Japan and later a full report in regard to the use of the money will be sent from Japan, and published in this paper.

ALICE MABEL BACON

4 Mansfield Street, New Haven, Conn.

(*New Haven Register*, January, 1905)

This article of Alice's had an immediate impact, and donations began to pour in. Alice forwarded them to Sutematsu, who sent a letter of thanks and a receipt to every one of the contributors. The total was not large, but represented to Sutematsu an important expression of the ties of friendship between the two nations. She thought long and hard about how to use the money, finally coming up with the following report, which she sent to Alice.

I have not written to you for a long time for one thing I have been extremely busy and for another I could not decide how to use your last gift to the best advantage. The 100 dollars is as exchanged to 202 yen and 53 sen. I gave 100 to Shige who has probably written to tell you how she disposed of the sum and I spent 2 yen and 53 sen for the comfort bags. It took me some time to decide in regard to the remaining 100 yen, but finally I divided it into two portions and gave 50 yen to the relief association of the village in which I live and the other 50 yen to a society which gives work to the families of those at the front. To the former I had given something last year myself, but the village is poor, and there are nearly 100 families which have to be looked after more or less by the village people themselves and as association needed urgent help, I thought it would not meet with your disapproval if I dispensed so much in this work.

As to the other, the society which gives work to families, it is doing splendid work, but also in need of money. It was started by some ten ladies last year and doing a great deal of good. The work is divided into two sections, one for sewing and the other for laundry. . . . If a woman can earn 15 sen a day, the society gives her perhaps 13 sen, and must keep the 2 sen to pay for a part of the running expenses. Of course that is not enough, and the expense of hiring the building, giving food, etc. must be paid by appeals to benevolent people. . . . In connection with this work, there is another section which is also very important and very interesting, and that is the place where little children are cared for while their mothers are at work. This branch is left in charge of four women themselves wives or mothers of soldiers, and one teacher. There are nearly fifty children of all ages, but they do not all come at once. . . . When I went to see the workings of the society, I saw some thirty children, two or three of whom must have been under a year old, and many of them five or six and all ages between. The teacher made the children sing the national anthem, and other songs which they did very well, and otherwise behaved very nicely. It is in reality a kindergarten with its scope enlarged. The teacher told me that when they were first brought there, they had no manners at all, and she had to teach them even to bow and say thank you, etc.

It made me a little sad to see them, for their little faces inevitably turned my mind to the thoughts of their fathers, some of whom had already died for their country and others are still fighting in Manchuria so far away and may perhaps never return to see their little ones. It occurred to me then that the gift of the High School Club could not be better used than giving a little pleasure to these destitute children, and so I told them if they are good and obeyed their teacher, I would give them a little treat out of the kind donation made by a school in America. When I wrote to you last, I thought of giving the High School Club money to a woman who is said to be taking care of the children of soldiers, but I could not find much about her, so I kept the money, and now I shall spend it in giving pleasure to these children, which can be done three or four times out of 10 yen.

May 17th. I had to leave it off yesterday as I had to go out, and just then your letter came enclosing a P.O. order for 106 dollars. Thank you so much for the repeated donations. It is a great privilege as well as a great pleasure for me to dispense these kind gifts of my American friends. I hope I am using them wisely.

(May 16–17, 1905)

Over thirty years after they had first met her, the residents of New Haven still remembered Sutematsu with affection. Now that lively young girl from the mysterious East was wife of the supreme commander of the army that had dared challenge the might of Russia, and the publication of her story in the local paper had resulted in donations from dozens of well-wishers, to Alice's delight.

All this was in glaring contrast with Japan, where neither Sutematsu's efforts nor the generosity of her American friends rated a mention in the papers. Today we think nothing unusual of day-care centers for working mothers, and the idea of arranging for families whose main breadwinner has died or been called up for military service, then subtracting a small sum from the income of the welfare organization for its running costs, does not shock us. At the time, however, those schemes for the dispersement of funds were nothing short of revolutionary—and were a credit to Sutematsu's genius. Her descriptions of the Japanese people uniting to fight for victory were the words of a patriot, but she went beyond words, brilliantly combining Japanese elements with American ways of thinking. In this way Sutematsu gave her heart and soul to the cause of her compatriots.

Following the victory at Mukden, Sutematsu took her pen and wrote to the American magazine *Collier's, The National Weekly.* P. F. Collier and Son Company was one of the most important publishing and newspaper companies in the United States. *Collier's* was a magazine read not so much by intellectuals as by the populace, and while it is not known exactly why Sutematsu chose it, there was no better way of informing the maximum number of people of the work being carried out behind the lines by Japanese women.

Sutematsu's writings were a persuasive and spirited appeal for readers' understanding and support. Lines appearing in *Collier's* such as "We are fighting for our very existence, and we know our cause is just and right" are reminiscent of the young Sutematsu at the siege of Tsuruga Castle. So determined was Sutematsu to make the people of her second home believe in the justice of the Japanese cause that Iwao Oyama, at army headquarters in Manchuria, was apparently concerned that his wife might give away classified information during one of her enthusiastic public relations exercises for Japan.

Although Sutematsu wrote in her article that Japan was prepared to fight for as many years as it took to achieve victory, her husband and the other government leaders had known since they entered the war that Japan did not have the strength for a prolonged conflict.

After a year and a half of fighting, with United States President Roosevelt acting as a mediator, Russia and Japan were finally able to sign the Portsmouth Treaty, bringing an end to the war on September 5, 1905. Japan failed to obtain reparations, but succeeded in all its other aims—gaining political, economic, and military rights in Korea, the lease of the Liaotung Peninsula and the Southern Manchuria branch of the East China Railway (with Chinese consent), fishing rights along the Russian coast of the Japan Sea, Sea of Okhotsk and Bering Sea, and possession of the southern half of Sakhalin. Success was not without cost though; Japan had lost 46,000 of its force of over a million, with another 153,000 wounded and 2,000 taken prisoner.

Interestingly, one of those who drafted the Portsmouth Treaty was Yale law professor Theodore Woolsey, brother-in-law of Alfred Bacon, Alice's elder brother. Another of her brothers, George Bacon, had visited Japan as a naval chaplain in 1856, only three years after Commodore Perry sailed his black ships into Uraga Bay. The Bacon family seemed to have many invisible ties with Japan, and one cannot help but feel that Sutematsu was predestined to live in their home.

On September 14, Iwao Oyama conveyed the news of the armistice to all the Japanese forces. He stayed in Manchuria himself for two months more, then on November 25 left Mukden, passing through Dairen and Port Arthur before arriving in Hiroshima on December 3, a year and a half after he had left Japan. In Hiroshima the Oyama's eldest son, Takashi, who had just entered the naval academy, was waiting, and the two greeted each other excitedly. Takashi was his parents' pride and joy. He had passed the entrance examination for the academy with excellent grades, and Sutematsu often spoke proudly of him in her letters to Alice.

On December 7, Oyama arrived at a rainy Shinbashi station in Tokyo on a special train set aside for the victorious returning soldiers, and from there proceeded to the imperial palace to report to the emperor, who had been eagerly awaiting his return. It wasn't until the completion of his duties at the palace that the general was finally able to head for home, where Sutematsu and other members of the family were waiting.

Though Sutematsu knew that her husband's high position safeguarded his life, upon seeing his face for the first time in well over a year she was overjoyed, and could feel the accumulated strain and worry of the past months suddenly dissolve from the depths of her being. Yet joy was not the only emotion she experienced—when Sutematsu thought of the tens of thousands of less fortunate families who had lost a husband, father, or son, she was overcome by complex feelings.

Autumn Years

PEACEFUL DAYS

With the war over and her husband home, life for Sutematsu settled into calmness again. Takashi was at the naval academy, the second son, Kashiwa, was in the army, and only the youngest child, Hisako, remained at home. Even during the hectic days of the war, Sutematsu had continued to assist Umeko Tsuda at her English school. In March 1904, under a new education law, her school was classified a "specialist school." Its image improved, and the number of students swelled to 180. In September of the same year, the school was incorporated. The property, buildings, and fittings, which until then had been in Umeko's name, became the property of the school, and Umeko and Sutematsu became the first directors.

The first meeting of a newly formed alumnae association was held on June 3, 1905, at which the sixty or so participants unanimously elected Sutematsu to the post of president. If she had played an important part in the progress of the school before, now she was indispensable.

By 1905 the school had produced thirty-one graduates. Slowly but surely Umeko's dream had begun to make an impact on women's education in Japan. Still, there was much to be done. As always, the school needed funds to buy land for new buildings and dormitories, to pay back loans, and to see to day-to-day administration. Once again Sutematsu led the way in fundraising, forming a committee for the purpose in March 1906 and holding the first meeting at her home. Over a six-year period, with the help of graduates and other benefactors, the committee raised fifteen thousand yen: enough to secure a plot of land the school had been planning to purchase for extensions.

Now approaching her fifties, Sutematsu entered the most peaceful and satisfying period of her life. Hisako had married, and the two boys were hardly at home, so life seemed unnaturally quiet compared with the earlier years of her marriage, when the house had been filled with the noise generated by six children. Yet, being able to spend so much time alone with her husband was a pleasant change for Sutematsu. She wrote to Alice:

> It is very difficult to begin a letter when one has been so remiss about correspondence as I have been. Before I say any thing else must thank you for the book which you sent me as a Xmas present. I received it a few days before I came here (Numazu) and so I brought it here to enjoy it in quiet. For the last two months I never was so busy in my life and I was so tired out that we came here to rest and enjoy a quiet life for two or three weeks. I never told you about Chachan's [Hisako's] engagement and her wedding, which took place on the 13th December. I am glad to tell you that her marriage is satisfactory in every way, and I think she will have a very happy life. The young man in question is an army officer, lieutenant, and he belongs to a very good family. His father was Baron Ida, and one time our minister to Austria and afterwards to France. The father being dead, he has a title,

and although not very rich, he has enough to live comfortably, according to Japanese standard. The young man is very steady and he quite distinguished himself in the late war and all the regimental officers speak of him as being a model officer. He does not drink and he does not smoke and he does not go to those horrid tea houses, which are often the ruin of young men. He is very quiet and rather shy, but you know Chachan is so lively and talkative that they suit each other very well indeed. They seem to be very much devoted to each other and are as happy as the day is long.

Of course I miss her dreadfully, but so long as she is happy, I do not complain. Very soon after her wedding, Takashi came back from the Naval Academy, so the house did not seem quite so empty, but he will have to go back tonight and there will be only Ojii san [old man] and Oba san [old woman] left again. Takashi, who used to give me so much anxiety, I am happy to say, has improved wonderfully and he is a great comfort to both myself and Marquis Oyama. He has grown so steady and thoughtful and is doing very well in his work. They tell me that he is very highly spoken of both by the teachers and pupils and that he is not at all like most of the sons of our upper classes, who have no idea of work and who spend lots of money and never understand what is expected of them. It is only one year more before he graduates and I am hoping that he will go on as he has begun.

Kashiwa, who used to be so delicate, is now quite strong, and though he has not the ability of his brother, he is a good boy and never gives me a cause for anxiety. In fact I feel very easy about all my children at present. I am very thankful that my life is so happy and peaceful. Marquis Oyama is very well and we lead quite a Darby and Joan existence.

I have been writing so much about myself and my affairs that I never asked how you were and all about yourself. . . .

I suppose you will see Ume this summer. You don't know

how glad we are that she is able to take such a long rest. It is so good of you to have sent the money which enabled her to take this trip without feeling anxious about her school. I am sure one year of rest will set her up again and she will be able to do twice the work after she returns. I don't know what we should have done if you did not help, for she was getting worse and worse and absolutely there was nothing to be done for her except her going away and taking a long rest.

(January 10, 1907)

In this letter Sutematsu writes of her concern for Umeko's health—in recent years the younger woman's asthma had taken a turn for the worse. The six years of unrelieved hard work to establish the school had also taken their toll. In January 1907, satisfied that the school was running smoothly, Umeko began a year's leave at the suggestion of Sutematsu and Shigeko, and traveled to Europe and the United States on a trip combining the inspection of various educational institutions with rest, hoping to recuperate from her illness. While she was away the post of director was filled by Anna Hartshorne, who had taken Alice's place in 1902. Sutematsu stood in for Umeko at the school's fifth graduation ceremony in March 1907.

Umeko journeyed first to Washington, where she met with Mrs. Lanman after an interval of nine years, then on to Alice's summer camp where she spent a relaxing few weeks. For many years Alice had dreamed of a place where people of all ethnic backgrounds and occupations could enjoy outdoor life and each other's company—where, as she saw it, they could appreciate the blessings that God had bestowed on them in the beautiful environment that He had created. In 1897, Alice was able to purchase a patch of land on the shore of Squam Lake in New Hampshire and build her camp, christening it "Deep Haven." Attracted by the warmth and humor of the owner as much as by the surroundings, college professors, scholars, and church workers gathered every summer to enjoy canoeing, picnics, and telling stories by the camp-fire. Japanese friends of Alice and Umeko were also frequent visi-tors, particularly students from Umeko's alma mater, Bryn Mawr College.

In the fall Umeko left New York to travel in southern Europe. She returned to Japan in January 1908, glowing with health and scarcely recognizable as the tired sickly woman who had left a year previously.

"GOD'S WILL BE DONE"

Overjoyed to see Umeko again, Sutematsu and Shigeko could not have known that shortly after their friend's return, fate would create a detour in their happy lives. By coincidence Sutematsu's and Shigeko's eldest sons were both in the navy and assigned to the same warship.

Sutematsu's son Takashi, a naval cadet, and Shigeko's son Takeo, a second lieutenant, were on an ocean voyage aboard the warship *Matsushima*. They had stopped at Singapore and Colombo, and were on their way home when disaster struck on April 30, 1908. While at anchor in the Pescadores, the gunpowder stored in the stern suddenly exploded, splitting the vessel in two and sending two hundred officers and men, including the captain, to their deaths.

Exceedingly proud of their beloved eldest son, the Oyamas had looked forward to his enjoyment of what would probably be a bril-liant career. Devastated by the death of their child, they withdrew to their summer holiday home at Nasuno, about 150 miles north of Tokyo, for a while. A month after her son's death Sutematsu was finally able to take up a pen again.

> Ume gave me your letter before I left Tokyo. It was a great comfort to receive such loving words. Many friends try to comfort me by saying that I have other children, but it is not that. I do not grieve for myself. It is the pity for the boy,

taken on the very threshold of life, with a brilliant future before him. At times I am very rebellious and say to myself, why should such a bright young life be taken, when there are others who could be better spared? But God's will be done and He knows what is best. I try not to grieve too much for if I give away [*sic*] too much to my feelings, it distresses my husband and adds to his sorrow and hurts Chachan's tender heart. It may be that the boy's death will not be in vain, for the authorities will try to find out the cause of explosion and so prevent future disasters of the kind and secure the safety of many lives.

You know Shige too has lost her eldest son, such a noble boy. She came up to Tokyo with the remains of all the officers, 45 in number, and the funeral services were held together at Aoyama cemetery. She came to see me for a few minutes, but probably I shall not see her again before she starts for Saseho. I shall return to Tokyo about the middle of this month and after staying for a few days, we think of going to Numazu for they all think it is best for both my husband and myself to be away in the country just as much as possible.

Now, dear Alice, don't be anxious about me. I am doing very well. I know my boy died the death he preferred—on board his ship. He had given his life to the services of his country and if he was cut off in the bloom of his youth, before he had achieved his purpose, his life however short would become a spur to others who are coming after him, for he combined all those qualities which make up a good naval officer and which are often lacking in the sons of our best families.

(June 8, 1908)

Following the Russo-Japanese War, Sutematsu and General Oyama spent an increasing amount of time at their country home in Nasuno, Tochigi Prefecture. In 1907, the year before the death of their son, Oyama was decorated with the Order of the Golden Kite, First Class, and his title upgraded to that of prince. Yet no matter what honors were bestowed on him or what rank he obtained, Iwao Oyama never altered his belief that military men should play no part in politics, and his dearest wish was to retire from the front lines of government decision-making as soon as possible and spend his days farming at Nasuno on a plot of land he had purchased with his cousin Tsugumichi Saigo. After all, he was sixty-seven years old by that time. The general spent what spare time he had on his land, planting trees and rice and communing with nature.

FAÇADE OF THE "NEW WOMEN"

For eight years following the death of Takashi no trace of any letters written by Sutematsu to Alice can be found. Since Sutematsu would not have suddenly broken off communications with her American friend, we can only assume that the correspondence was lost.

On July 30, 1912, the Meiji emperor died, and with the new emperor the era name changed from Meiji to Taisho. In the short forty-five years of the Meiji period, Japan had risen from feudal obscurity and isolationism to stand among the great powers of the world and defeat its giant neighbor Russia in the Russo-Japanese War. Over forty years had passed since five young Japanese girls had boarded the *America* for their voyage across the Pacific with the Iwakura Mission.

The tenth anniversary celebrations for Umeko's English school had taken place the previous year. Eighty young women had graduated from the school and ventured out into society. Of those graduates, fifty had taken up teaching positions, and while small in number, their efforts gradually brought the profession of English teaching the recognition and respect it was due.

In April 1916, the first happy event in quite some time took place in the Oyama household—the marriage of second son and now family heir Kashiwa. His bride was Takeko Konoe. The Konoes were old court nobles of Kyoto who had brought their children up according to traditions passed down over the generations, so to poor Takeko the move into the Oyama's Westernized, fashionable home was not unlike traveling to a foreign country. But the girl cheerfully adapted to her husband's family, and Sutematsu soon became fond of the young girl, her first and only daughter-in-law. Takeko was later heard to comment that when she agreed to marry Kashiwa Oyama those around her had conjured up visions of that notorious novel *Hototogisu* and warned her that she would be mistreated by her mother-in-law. However, when she actually went to live with the Oyamas, she found Sutematsu to be generous and broad-minded, very different from the way she was portrayed in the novel, and she counted herself very lucky.

> It is a long time since I have written to you. . . .
>
> As to my family, we are all well. Kashiwa was married last year and the young people are living with us. The bride is the sister of Prince Konoe, one of the oldest families in Japan. Though she is not pretty, she has a lovely disposition, for she has been brought up in an old fashioned way by her mother, and is just as sweet and good as possible.
>
> I am sorry to say young girls nowadays are not like what they used to be. They have lost the best characteristics of Japanese women without gaining the best side of foreign education. It may be that I am rather old fashioned, but it seems to me that female education in Japan is not advancing in the right direction.
>
> When are you coming again to Japan? I heard some one say that you thought of coming over at no distant future.
>
> (March 12, 1912)

In this letter Sutematsu, obviously concerned that women's education was beginning to follow an undesirable path, laments the disappearance of the type of femininity that Japanese women had traditionally regarded as a virtue. While it is unclear precisely which modern customs Sutematsu is criticizing, the period from the end of the Meiji era to the beginning of Taisho saw the publication of the literary magazine *Seito* (*Bluestocking*), put out by a new breed of women writers waking up to their rights.

Raicho Hiratsuka, one of the publishers, was a graduate of the Japan Women's University, the nation's first such institution, founded by Jinzo Narese in 1901. In the first issue of *Seito* she challenged her countrywomen, ". . . In ancient times woman was the sun. She was genuine. Now woman is the moon. She exists only in the shadow of man, and shines only from the reflected light of her master. She is like the pallid, sickly moon. We must make this sun which is hidden within all of us shine once more."

The call of Raicho Hiratsuka and others for women to break free of their traditional bonds and make use of the abilities they were born with opened a floodgate, and one after the other female authors as well as anonymous women sent their writings to be published in *Seito*. The magazine later began to tackle social issues, and eventually progressed to become the New Women's Association, an organization that fought for women's suffrage and came to have considerable political clout.

To much of Japanese society, however, these women were regarded as having overstepped the mark in their pursuit of, among other things, free love, and were the target of frequent and virulent criticism. To Sutematsu, who had been raised for so many years in the conservative Puritan atmosphere of the Bacon household, the lifestyle these "new women" promoted must have seemed a superficial and mistaken adaptation of Western ideas of equality between men and women.

After the promulgation of the Act of Girls' High Schools, there had undoubtedly been a leap in the number of such institutions for girls, with 133 schools registered by 1907. But closer examination reveals that at the time of the Russo-Japanese War the trend in women's education had actually moved away from the Western-style schools of the earlier *bunmei kaika* ("civilization and enlightenment") period, during which the government was promoting all-out Westernization, back to the pre-Restoration concept of educating girls to be "good wives and wise mothers." Certainly the fact that higher education for women even existed was an improvement on what the situation had been when Sutematsu returned from the United States, but the vast majority of the institutions placed a great deal more emphasis on moral education, sewing, and housekeeping than on any academic subject. Apart from Women's Higher Normal School, which trained teachers, there was not a single public school concentrating on vocational subjects, and only two such private schools: Umeko's and the Tokyo Women's Medical School founded by Yayoi Yoshioka.

Not surprisingly, Sutematsu was disturbed by the trend toward tying women to the home again. Umeko's school was really the only hope for women's education, she reasoned, and worked tirelessly by her friend's side for its advancement.

SUTEMATSU'S "ONE GREAT COMFORT"

In September 1916, Kashiwa's wife, Takeko, gave birth to a boy. At last there was a child to carry on the family name, and the doting grandparents were thrilled.

On November 17, Oyama accompanied the emperor to observe large-scale military maneuvers taking place in Kyushu, southernmost of the main Japanese islands. On the return journey, as the train pulled into Suma near Osaka, the general suddenly doubled over with pain. He was quickly taken home and diagnosed with inflammation of the gallbladder. Day and night Oyama was attended by the best medical doctors in the country as well as by Sutematsu and his three daughters, who had rushed home to nurse their father. The emperor showed his concern by dispatching his personal doctor to the Oyama home. He also sent frequent messengers with gifts, including a supply of soup for the ailing general. Despite all this loving attention, seventy-five-year-old comatose Oyama was too weak to fight the illness and on December 10 he quietly breathed his last.

The government called an emergency cabinet meeting the following day and decided to give General Oyama a state funeral. General Kuroki, commander of the First Army during the Russo-Japanese War, was given the task of organizing it. On the afternoon of December 13, the body was removed from the Western-style wing of the house to the large Japanese-style meeting room, where it was layed in a coffin. Carrying his father's beloved sword aloft in a final salute, Kashiwa, the chief mourner, walked behind the casket, followed by Sutematsu. She was dressed in mourning, and the hair she had kept in a fringe for forty years was tied tightly back in a bun. From that point on, the funeral of Iwao Oyama ceased to be a family affair and was conducted by the state.

Early on the morning of the seventeenth a farewell ceremony for the deceased was held. At seven-thirty the hearse left the Oyama home for Hibiya in Tokyo, preceded by a contingent of mounted police. Unable to contain their grief, Oyama's three daughters wept copiously, covering their faces, but Sutematsu simply gazed in silence at her husband's coffin as it disappeared into the distance.

The funeral procession followed a tortuous path of almost five miles to the athletic grounds situated near the Diet buildings. Here, the official funeral ceremony took place. Black and white banners bedecked the grounds, and on the white sand spread for the occasion a forest of *sakaki* (sacred trees) sprouted. The sakaki were funeral offerings from the imperial families, and there were also wreaths sent by foreign legations. Sutematsu, who was there to greet the coffin when it arrived, sat dry-eyed and silent with her head bowed down throughout the service, her only discernible movement a slight quiver of the fan that she held.

Following the service Oyama's body was carried to Ueno Station, from where it traveled to the Oyama's country house at Nasuno. It had been the general's wish that he be buried in the hills to the north of their residence, with a view of the nearby Japanese cypress trees. By the time the coffin arrived at Nasuno it was dark, but the villagers had gathered at the station to pay their last respects to the great benefactor who had transformed the wilderness into a beautiful green forest. The coffin was unloaded from the train and carried through the silent crowd of mourners—many of whom held lanterns in their hands—to the Oyama residence. The burial took place the following morning, when a pulley lowered the general's coffin deep into a massive grave that was still in the midst of construction. Using a hoe, Kashiwa sprinkled earth on the coffin, followed by a shaking Sutematsu.

After their return to Tokyo, the family had to attend further Shinto ceremonies of the type associated with state funerals, and it was not until March 1917 that Sutematsu was able to take up her pen to write to Alice.

> You must forgive me for the great delay in answering your letter. There was so much to do that I could not sit down to write without constant interruptions and so I gave up letter writing until nearly all the business was done away with. Being so busy, however, kept me from thinking and dwelling on the past, which all my friends said was the best thing for me. You have no idea of the things that have to be thought of, and done after a Japanese funeral, especially if it is a state funeral.
>
> There is no use in telling you of all that the loss of my husband means to me, but there has been one great comfort in the thought that he died while in actual service to the Emperor. You know he accompanied His Majesty to the Grand Maneuvers and it was during the return journey he contracted his mortal illness and died after less than three weeks after his return home.
>
> He had the best medical advice, for we had not only three

or four doctors who stayed with him day and night, but the Emperor send [*sic*] every day Dr. Miura who is considered the most skilled physician in Japan. Every thing was done but his age told against him. There was another thing that I am always glad to think of, that was he lived to see his grandson. It had been a great joy to him that Kashiwa had a son, for that will ensure the succession, and nothing gave him so much pleasure as to bring the baby into the sick room for a few minutes.

I shall continue to live with Kashiwa and his wife and we shall be soon settled into new order of things. I wish you would come again to Japan. Ume was telling me that you thought of coming over some time. If so, you need not fear that you will not receive a hearty welcome, for you have many friends in Japan who would be more than glad to see you again. Do come. . . .

(March 10, 1917)

Following her husband's death, Sutematsu withdrew from public life completely, sending her daughter-in-law Takeko in her place to perform the various social duties she had taken on over the years. Japan had already declared war on Germany in World War I when the above letter was written, and in August 1918 sent troops to the frozen wastes of Siberia. Once again the upper-class ladies of Tokyo gathered at the Red Cross hospital to roll bandages; however, Sutematsu sent Takeko to the meetings this time and confined herself to forming a group of American wives who knitted clothes for the troops overseas—a far cry from her impassioned involvement during the Russo-Japanese War.

Sutematsu's greatest pleasure in life now was the company of her two grandchildren. As she remarked to friends, when she was with them the days seemed to fly by. In this picture of a doting grandmother enjoying the joys and sorrows of her grandchildren growing up, there is no trace to be seen of one of Japan's first female students to study abroad, nor of the wife of a prominent government official, the labels she had borne for forty years.

FAREWELL TO "DEAR ALICE"

Although Sutematsu no longer took part in social functions, there was one type of work that she threw herself into with all the old enthusiasm—that which involved her responsibilities as a director of Umeko's English school. Through her friend's success, Sutematsu in a sense, lived the dream of having her own school, a vision she had given up when she married Iwao Oyama.

Like Umeko, Sutematsu believed women were naturally endowed with a talent for teaching. Remaining uninfluenced by the "new women" of the *Seito* strain, they continued to run the school in line with their original formula of simplicity without pretension, and with a dedication to freedom of expression. The number of hopefuls wishing to enter the school increased annually: in 1916 there were ninety-five first-year students, twice the number of any previous year.

The school was progressing in leaps and bounds. Sutematsu turned her attention to Umeko's health, and the appointment of her successor as principal. At one stage Umeko appeared to have recovered her health, but in the spring of 1917 she fell ill again. At the hospital she was found to be suffering from diabetes. Once diagnosed her recovery was slower than expected and she spent the remainder of the year being admitted and readmitted to the hospital. She did recover sufficiently to accept Sutematsu's invitation to convalesce in Numazu, whose climate was warmer than Tokyo's, but Sutematsu knew that the time had come to select a new principal. She wrote to Alice for advice.

I met Hitotsuyanagi [Makiko; one of Alice's adopted daughters] some time ago at Ume's and she gave me your letter. The book which you were so good as to send me has not come but she thinks it will come by and by. I was so glad to meet her and hear the latest news of the Bacon family. I hope I shall see her again very soon and hear more about them, for the talk we had the other day was not sufficient to satisfy my craving to hear all about the Bacons and New Haven.

She is a charming girl and gives me the impression of great capability. We are hoping that when she comes back to Japan, she will be persuaded to take Ume's place. You know about Ume's illness. I do not think she will ever be able to work as she used to do and there is no one to take her place, at least there is no one to whom we are willing to offer the place. Miss Hitotsuyanagi is just the person and I think she will do even better than Ume, as she has better Japanese education. I do wish you would persuade her to do so. Can't you come over with her and help her with your advice, etc. We have been quite worried about Ume, not that she is worse, but she does not improve. If only she could feel quite easy about the school, I think she might recover at least a part of her health, though it is quite hopeless to think that she will ever be strong again.

Thank you so much for what you have done for my nephew. Miss Hitotsuyanagi told me all about it.

My family are all well. Did I tell you that I have another grandson? Of course when two babies are in the house, there is always some ailment or another but nothing serious. They are a great joy and pleasure to me, especially the elder boy, as he is now learning to talk.

(February 17, 1918)

After thirty-six years of correspondence, this was to be the last letter Sutematsu would write with the opening "Dear Alice." In May of the same year, her friend of almost half a century succumbed to an intestinal ailment, passing away at the age of sixty-one in her hometown of New Haven.

Of the Bacon children Alice had been the closest in age to

Sutematsu and had had the greatest effect on her Japanese sister's life. It was through Alice that the young girl from the land of the Mikado with barely adequate English was able to enter the exclusive upper-class society of New Haven, and the things that Sutematsu learned in that milieu proved to be invaluable in later life. It was the example of Alice dedicating herself to the education of black Americans from an early age, under the influence of her father's views on race issues, that gave Sutematsu the idea of opening her own school and working for the cause of women's education in Japan. Although Sutematsu never realized the dream of her own school, at the crucial beginnings of the Peeresses' School, Women's Higher Normal School, and Umeko's Joshi Eigakujuku—all pioneering educational institutions for women—she was able to enlist Alice's assistance as a skilled educator and work with her to get each school established.

The influence was not entirely one-way, for Alice's encounter with Sutematsu, Umeko, and Shigeko was to change her life. Twice she crossed the Pacific to answer her friends' calls, sacrificing her own work in the process. And through her contact with Japan, Alice acquired two young Japanese girls as adopted daughters. Alice, who remained single all her life, was grateful to the girls for easing the loneliness she sometimes felt, and was fiercely attached to them. One of the girls was Mitsuko Watanabe, whom Alice had taken back to the United States after her first trip to Japan. Mitsuko was five at the time, and she remained in Alice's care for twelve years. Alice brought the girl back to Japan on her second trip, and deciding that Mitsuko could cope with Japanese life, left her behind to teach at Umeko's school, requesting that Sutematsu, Umeko, and Shigeko become her "parents." Three years later Mitsuko entered into a happy marriage.

The other girl was Makiko Hitotsuyanagi, whose first encounter with Alice was as her pupil of English conversation in Japan. Disillusioned by the fact that daughters of the upper class generally married at once and became housewives when they left school, Makiko pleaded with her father to allow her to travel to the United States. He gave his permission reluctantly, and she entered Bryn Mawr College in September 1912 as a special student. But a bout of typhoid forced her to discontinue her studies, and Makiko fell into a deep depression. Then Alice stepped in, extending a helping hand. Between the woman with no children of her own and the girl who had lost her mother at a young age a close relationship evolved, and Alice hardly let Makiko out of her sight, enlisting her help in administering the summer camp at Deep Haven. Following Alice's death, Makiko tidied up various matters of the estate and returned to Japan. She turned down the position of principal of Umeko's English school, opting, instead, to marry American architect Merrell Vories, designer of the Meiji Gakuen chapel and a number of other Western-style buildings in Tokyo, and work with him in his business.

Alice willed her New Haven home and the Deep Haven camp to her two Japanese daughters, and requested that they in turn will the properties to the Hampton Institute at which she had taught. The pioneering educator was laid to rest next to her father, the Reverend Leonard Bacon, in a grave behind Yale University.

Alice's death left a lonely gap in the lives of Sutematsu and Umeko. Altogether, Alice had spent only three years in Japan, but over the years the two Japanese women had found a great source of strength in knowing they had a friend across the Pacific who was as concerned as they were about the future of women's education in their country. Sutematsu in particular had found comfort in writing to Alice whenever she felt lonely or troubled. It was painful to know that her request to her American sister to come to Japan once more for Umeko's sake would never be fulfilled, and that she would never see Alice again.

THE FINAL TASK

Toward the end of the same year Umeko's condition deteriorated once again, forcing her to return to the hospital. In January

1919 she tendered her resignation, explaining to Sutematsu and the other directors that she could no longer continue working. An emergency meeting was called at which the directors asked Matsu Tsuji, who had been teaching English-to-Japanese translation for three years, to accept the post of principal. Tsuji asked for time to consider the offer and the meeting broke up with the issue left unresolved.

Around that time a virulent virus known as the Spanish flu was forcing many Tokyo residents to take to their beds, including many of the Oyama household staff and live-in students. Fearing that the grandchildren would be infected, Sutematsu took the family to the residence at Numazu to wait for the virus to disappear from the capital. But she was restless there, as the problem of Umeko's successor had not been solved, and she returned to Tokyo by herself. It was hardly surprising that Sutematsu, surrounded by infected servants, soon became ill herself. In the meantime Matsu Tsuji had given a negative answer: while she found her role as teacher fulfilling, she explained, she had absolutely no interest in the administrative post of principal. Desperate on account of Umeko and the future of the school, Sutematsu dragged her weakened body to Tsuji's home and pleaded with the teacher. Tsuji finally relented and agreed to take on the position, but only until someone else could be found.

On February 5 Matsu Tsuji was temporarily installed in the post of principal. Sutematsu attended the ceremony with a great sense of relief, feeling that she had carried out her responsibility as a director and as a friend of Umeko. It was to be the last time anyone saw Sutematsu in reasonable health. The following morning she woke up with a severe sore throat, and stayed in bed. After a few days of rest she appeared on her way to recovery, but then suffered a burning fever followed by pneumonia. On the morning of February 18, Sutematsu's condition took a sudden turn for the worse; she began to experience difficulty in breathing, and at around four o'clock in the afternoon she passed away. She was sixty years old.

A doctor had injected Sutematsu with a vaccine immediately before she died. Her daughter-in-law, Takeko, later remembered that the color of Sutematsu's face had changed and her body shook as the doctor was performing the injection. Since Sutematsu was prone to allergies, it is possible that the vaccine hastened her death.

Four days later a quiet farewell ceremony was held at the Oyama home amid pouring rain. In accordance with Sutematsu's wishes the funeral was neither Buddhist nor Shinto. As the mourners filed past the coffin, each placed a flower on it as they prayed for their friend's safe passage into the next world. The sight of Umeko, who had made the gargantuan effort of leaving her sickbed to bid farewell to her dearest friend, filled the gathering with even more sadness. The loss of the woman she had loved like a sister for fifty years hit Umeko hard, particularly when she had only recently lost another friend, Alice, who had always supported and encouraged her in her work with the English school.

The next day a train carried Sutematsu to Nasuno, to her final resting place by her husband.

Sutematsu's life was influenced by the historical events of the Meiji period to an extent that perhaps even she herself was not aware of. For Japan to be freed from its self-imposed isolation and become a member of the international community, it had to pass through different stages of development. Those stages may be identified as the Aizu War, the dispatch of the Iwakura Mission the United States to and Europe, the Rokumeikan Era—which typified the Westernization policy at its most extreme—and the wars with China and Russia for rights on the continent. Interestingly enough, Sutematsu was deeply involved in every one of those epoch-making events. Through them all she was cast as the "First

Lady," playing each scene to the very best of her ability.

When Sutematsu returned to Japan after eleven years in the United States, she found a society still unprepared to accept women who chose to work rather than marry. Sutematsu chose marriage to a high-ranking government official in the hope that once she became the wife of such a man, she could use her talents to fulfill some of the aims she held dear. It was a decision based on logic typical of Sutematsu, and no doubt many things she achieved would not have been possible without her husband's position in society.

On the other hand, in consigning herself to the position of an upper-class wife, the girl who had enjoyed such a carefree existence in America was in reality condemning herself to a very restricted lifestyle—one which often stifled rather than made the most of her abilities. Did Sutematsu herself realize the irony of her choice?

Sutematsu's American friend Marian Whitney, who visited Japan just before the outbreak of the Russo-Japanese War, hit the nail firmly on the head regarding Sutematsu's lifestyle, in an article in the *Vassar Quarterly* of July 1919.

> Madame Oyama herself told me that it was often hard not to join in general conversation on public affairs in which she was so deeply interested, but it would not have done at all for her to do so in society—it would have been contrary to all etiquette. . . .
>
> We had hardly arrived at our hotel at Tokio when the Marchioness appeared to welcome us and it needed only the impression which her coming made on the hotel personnel to show us what a very great lady she was. We found her the same charming friend and comrade, as graceful as ever in her Japanese dress of soft, dull gray crêpe, but older, we felt, than she ought to be. And after an hour together, talking over old times and the humors of our voyage, she said: "I haven't

laughed so much for years. In Japan we do not laugh much after we are old women." . . .

We made various expeditions together during the few weeks we were in Tokio. One long day we spent with Madame Oyama and Madame Uriu in the Imperial Gardens, lunching from one of those wonderful Japanese lacquer picnic boxes with their many compartments and talking over with the utmost frankness all the problems of politics, education and social life, both American and Japanese, which would naturally present themselves to such a group of friends. I was struck with the breadth and fairness of Madame Oyama's outlook and with her lack of prejudice, while her intimate knowledge of both the American and Japanese point of view made her a wonderful guide to us in understanding her country. I thought at the time that Japanese society must lose a good deal by condemning such a spirit to the role of silent onlooker or indirect influence, when she should have been openly a leader in all good things.

Sutematsu had always wanted to visit the United States once again before she died: to see Washington, where she and the other girls had spent their "golden days," to wander through New Haven, her second home, and to visit the campus at Vassar where she had spun the dreams of her youth. However, as the wife of a high-ranking member of the government she was restricted even in her movements within Japan, and embarking on a trip overseas by herself was unthinkable. In any case Sutematsu knew that an endless succession of elaborate receptions awaited her at every destination, and this, she intimated to Marian, combined with the necessity of staying in the kind of expensive places deemed appropriate to her station, was enough in itself to discourage her from traveling either at home or abroad.

For the same reason she did not often visit the theater, where her rank required her to occupy an expensive box and give handsome fees to the attendants. She agreed to go with us one night "incognito," thinking she would not be recognized in the background of our little box, but before the performance was over the proprietor and his wife appeared, prostrating themselves at her feet, protesting their horror that they had not done proper honor to so lofty a personage, who should have had the best place in their humble theater, etc. Madame Oyama was half amused and half distressed but she would not go with us again.

(*Vassar Quarterly*, July 1919)

That artless young girl happily jumping off bridges and climbing trees in New Haven, who on returning to Japan found herself so bound by convention and tradition that she forgot what it was like to laugh for more than a moment—whose heart would not go out to her? It was to be many years before Japan was prepared to allow women like Sutematsu to express themselves freely without fear of censure.

Bibliography

Adachi, Yoshio. *Aizu Tsurugajo no onnatachi*. Rekishi Shunjusha, 1981.

Aizu Shidankai. *Aizu senso no subete*. Shinjinbutsu Oraisha, 1980.

Bäelze, Toku, ed. *Bäelze no nikki*. Translated by Suganuma Ryutaro. Vol. 1. Iwanami Shoten, 1979.

Bessatsu rekishi tokuhon. *Meiji, Taisho o ikita jugonin no onnatachi*. Shinjinbutsu Oraisha, 1980.

Dulles, Foster Rhea. *Samurai to Yanki*. Translated by Sakurada Masako et al. Yomiuri Shinbunsha, 1969.

Haga, Toru. *Taikun no shisetsu*. Chukoshinsho, 1968.

Hakodateshi. *Hakodateshishi*. Vols. 1 and 2. Shiryohen, 1974.

Hanabusa, Nagamichi. *Meiji gaikoshi*. Nihon Rekishi Shinsho, 1960.

Hiraishi, Benzo. *Aizu Boshin senso zoho Byakkotai joshi koreisha no kento*. Maruhachi Shoten Publishers, 1937.

Ishikawa, Kisaburo. *Nihon seikyo dendoshi*. Seikyokai Hensankyoku, 1901.

Ishimitsu, Mahito. *Aru Meijijin no kiroku: Aizujin Shiba Goro no yuigon*. Chuokoronsha, 1971.

Ishizuki, Minoru. *Kindai Nihon no kaigai ryugakushi*. Minerva Shobo, 1972.

Iwasaki, Kyoko. *Shojotachi no Meiji ishin*. PHP Kenkyusho, 1983.

Joseishi Sogo Kenkyukai. *Nihon joseishi*. Vol. 4, Kindai. Tokyo Daigaku Shuppankai, 1982.

Kaigo, Muneomi, and Kishimoto, Hideo. *Nichibei bunka koshoshi*. Vol. 3. Yoyosha, 1956.

Kajiwara, Kagehiro. *Kajiwara Kagehiro ikoshu—Aizu no hito*. Yaedake Shobo, 1980.

Kameyama, Michiko. *Kindai Nihon kangoshi*. Domesu Shuppan, 1983.

Kamigaito, Kenichi. *Ishin no ryugakusei.* Shufunotomosha, 1971.

Kasai, Tomio. *Tonami Hanshi.* Tonami Aizukai, 1971.

Kimura, Tsuyoshi. *Kaigai ni katsuyaku shita Meiji no josei.* Nihon Rekishi Shinsho, 1963.

Kimura, Tsuyoshi. *Oyama Gensui.* Dai Nihon Yubenkai Kodansha, 1942.

Kojima, Noboru. *Oyama Iwao 1, 2, 3, 4.* Bungei Shunjusha, 1977.

Kondo, Tomie. *Rokumeikan Kifujin ko.* Kodansha, 1980.

Kume, Kunitake, ed. *Beio kairan jikki.* Revised by Tanaka Akira. Vol. 1. Iwanami Shoten, 1977.

Miyamoto, Takashi. *Peri teitoku.* Yurin Shinsho, 1981.

Miyazaki, Tomihachi. "Yamakawa Sutematsu no hikari to kage." *Rekishi Shunju,* no. 13. Aizu Shigakkai, 1981.

Morimoto, Sadako. *Onna no kaiko—Tone Mirun no seishun.* Bungei Shunjusha, 1981.

Musashi Kotogakko Koyukai. *Yamakawa Rosensei (Kenjiro Danshaku) Rokujunen mae gaiyu no omoide.* Koyukai, 1931.

Nishio, Hosaku. *Shimoda Utako den.* Kosaijuku, 1936.

Oba, Minako. *Tsuda Umeko.* Asahi Shinbunsha, 1990.

Okubo, Toshiaki. *Mori Arinori zenshu.* Senbundo Shoten, 1972.

Ono, Tadaakira, ed. *Kita Nihon Katorikku kyokaishi, jinbutsu, kyokai, iseki.* Chuo Shuppansha, 1970.

Oyama, Kashiwa. *Boshin Eki Senso.* Vols. 1 and 2. Jiji Tsushinsha, 1968.

Sakurai, Mamoru. *Joshi kyoikushi.* Zoshindo, 1943.

Shiba, Ryotaro. *Ojo no goeisha.* Kodansha, 1971.

Shimizu, Hiroshi, ed. *Amerikashi.* Yamakawa Shuppansha, 1955.

Shinoda, Kozo. *Bakumatsu Meiji onna hyakubanashi.* Kadokawa Shoten, 1971.

Shiotani, Shichijuro. *Hanitsu Jinja keidai "Chukonhi" ni tsuite.* Vol. 14. Inawashiro Chihoshi Kenkyukaishi, 1981.

Tanaka, Akira. *Iwakura shisetsudan.* Kodansha Gendai Shinsho, 1977.

Tokutomi, Roka. *Hototogisu.* Iwanami Shoten, 1938.

Tsudajuku Daigaku. *Tsudajuku rokujunenshi.* Tsudajuku Daigaku, 1970.

Umetani, Noboru. *Oyatoi gaikokujin.* Vol. 1, Introduction. Kajima Shuppankai, 1979.

Yamaguchi, Reiko. *Tokuto ware o mitamae: Wakamatsu Shizuko no shogai.* Shinchosha, 1980.

Yamazaki, Takako. *Tsuda Umeko.* Yoshikawa Kobunkan, 1962.

Bacon, Alice Mabel. *A Japanese Interior.* Boston and New York: Houghton, Mifflin and Co., 1894.

Bacon, Benjamin W. *Leonard Bacon.* New Haven: Yale University Press, 1931.

Bacon, Marion. *Life at Vassar.* Poughkeepsie: Vassar Cooperative Bookshop, 1940.

Fletcher, Grace N. *The Bridge of Love.* New York: E. P. Dutton & Co., 1967.

Furuki, Yoshiko et al., eds. *The Attic Letters.* New York: Weatherhill, 1991.

Griffis, William Elliot. *The Rutgers Graduates in Japan.* New Brunswick: Rutgers College, 1885.

Heinz, Bernard. *Center Church on-the-Green.* New Haven: Bruce Mochan, 1976.

Howe, Henry. *Outline History of New Haven.* New Haven: The Manufacturing Stationer, 1884.

Lanman, Charles. *Japanese in America.* New York: University Publishing Co., 1872.

Osterweis, Rollin G. *Three Centuries of New Haven.* New Haven: Yale University Press, 1953.

Reischauer, Haru Matsukata. *Samurai and Silk.* Cambridge, Mass.: Belknap Press of Harvard University Press, 1986.

Rukeyser, Muriel. *Willard Gibbs.* New York: Doubleday Doran, 1942.

Treat, Payson J. *Diplomatic Relations between the United States and Japan.* California: Stanford University Press, 1932.

Vassar College. *The Magnificent Enterprise.* Poughkeepsie: Vassar Cooperative Bookshop, 1961.

Whitney, Clara. *Clara's Diary.* Tokyo: Kodansha International, 1981.

The Bacon Family Documents, Manuscripts, and Archives,
   Yale University.

San Francisco Examiner, Jan. 15–24, 1872.

San Francisco Bulletin, Jan. 15–25, 1872.

The Daily Morning Call, Jan. 16–25, 1872.

The Daily Evening Bulletin, Jan. 17–23, 1872.

Washington Chronicles, March 1, 1872.

The Evening Star, March 2–5, 1872.

Frank Leslie's Illustrated Newspaper, March 23, 1872.

Poughkeepsie Eagle, June 15, 1882.

The Independent, April, 1883, January, 1896.

Vassar Miscellany, February, 1901.

Records of The Class of '82, Vassar College, 1902.

The Twentieth Century Home, 1904.

New Haven Register, January, 1905.

Collier's, The National Weekly, April 1, 1905.